Praying T Psalms

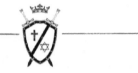

A New Covenant approach to praying the Psalms

Yearning for God in Times of Despair

By: Michael S. Wolff

PRAYING TODAY'S PSALMS: YEARNING FOR GOD IN TIMES OF DESPAIR
Published by: Reconnections, Inc.
ISBN# 979-8-9863874-6-8
Copyright © 2023 by Michael Wolff

Cover design by Elaina Lee
Available in print from your local bookstore, online, or at www.
Theawakenedchrisitanman.org
For more information on this book and the author, contact him at
Reconnectedchurch@gmail.com

Library of Congress Cataloging-in-Publication Data
Wolff, Michael
Praying Today's Psalms: Psalms of Yearning / Mike Wolff 2nd ed.
Printed in the United States of America

Praise for Praying Today's Psalms

I no longer seek knowledge, for knowledge is too easily gained and one can do so without what they study transforming them in any significant way. I seek revelation, for that is a gift of God that is personal and always transforms me. When I pray the psalms in Mike's devotional, I get revelation!

Michael Wells
Director, Abiding Life Ministries International

Mike Wolff has a way of leading one to pray the Psalms in a unique way, which has become my practice since I read his first book about it. I also have learned to pray other Scriptures. Praying this way has enlightened me and added depth to my prayer life and my journaling, as well as opening up the Scriptures in a fresh way. I have been sharing this practice with a group of ladies in a Bible study setting, and it has been very helpful to all of them as well.

Jeanne Stone Helstrom
Author

The Psalms are so personal to David and other psalmists. Praying Today's Psalms made them personal for me. This devotional book helped me to see the Scriptures in a whole new light. My conversation with God is more intimate, and my spirit is renewed when I pray the Psalms and make them my own. Mike's "newtestamentizing" them, as he calls it, made it possible for one like me living under the new covenant to do that.

Cherrilynn Bisbano
Associate Editor

Table of Contents

Introduction 6

Index by Subtitles 15

The Devotional Entries 19

About the Psalms 127

Inescapable callings..147

Epilogue 166

Appendage: References to
Fearing God in the Psalms 169

Introduction

It has often been said that if we want to hook up with God, we should seek to find the place where He is already working and join Him. Putting my once dysfunctional journey of prayer behind me, I found this is truer nowhere than joining Him in an old thing: praying the Psalms! For many years I struggled with focus in my prayers, and I didn't have a gift of intercession. I suffered mightily from a disease I came to describe as "Mindusconstantwanderitis."

It didn't help at all that I talk to myself a lot, because I would begin my prayers in a relatively focused way, and yet within a few minutes find myself talking to myself rather than God. I would be found soundly rebuking one of my sons for some crime against parenthood or setting up a two-way between myself and a business associate I was dealing with. Suddenly I would recover and reel myself back in, only to be drawn into the whole sordid process all over again. I think most men struggle with prayer, either vainly flitting from prayer formula to prayer formula, resigning themselves to a life of talking to the sky, or pretty much giving up altogether.

It would seem one of the most famous devotional writers who ever lived shared my disease. In his timeless devotional, *My Utmost for His Highest*, Oswald Chambers says:

> We cannot seem to get our minds into good working order, and the first thing we have to fight is wandering thoughts. The great battle in private prayer is overcoming this problem of our idle and wandering thinking.

Oh, what to do?

Then, at a men's retreat high in the mountains of Colorado, still hopelessly locked in my prayer struggles, I was first introduced to the concept of praying the Psalms. "What did I have to lose?" I asked myself [remember—talking to myself?]. Absolutely nothing. Things couldn't have been any worse, so I decided to give it a try. As I took my first baby-steps into a wholly different experience, I found the Psalms to be a totally unique book among all of the Scriptures because it was the only one that actually invited me into a relationship between a somewhat unknowable God and passionate followers diligently seeking to bridge the gap. It didn't just tell me stories about a great God and great men of faith, it invited me into the conversation so I could become a part of it.

The speaker that weekend talked of how praying with God through the Psalms could introduce passion and focus into my prayers. Who, me? I later came to give that one a checkmark. He said the practice could help me confront God with integrity during times when I questioned what He was doing in my life. Another checkmark. He said my focus could be maintained as I prayed because it would be God leading, and not me. Triple-check and checkmate!

These magical song-prayers take you to unscalable heights and through desperate, endless valleys. They make you part of the scene because they are prayers written in the first-person by flawed human beings you can relate to, yet who are striving to connect just as you are. They delve into the depths of human joy, suffering, and pain like no other book of the Bible. Perhaps this is why you will find those who write books about their personal struggles inevitably wind up talking about the Psalms. This unique approach has made the Psalms the endearing, healing source for many who have suffered over the centuries. It has also made praying the Psalms a primary discipline for ascetics in monasteries around the world.

After God revealed to me I could overcome the obstacles Old Covenant thought presented to praying as a Christian [read on], I can now start my day by going to my loving, and yet somewhat unknowable, God via the prayers He has already written. I can now join my spirit to His in a depth of relationship I don't believe I would have otherwise known.

If your prayer life is like mine was, it can be transformed as mine was through praying with passionate "men after God's own heart." And isn't that what we want, to reach the heart of God through our prayers? And even if you have a rich prayer life, it can be made all the richer. I hope you will use this devotional to regularly join God in the prayer-thing He set up thousands of years ago. If you will, it can be a real game-changer!

"Newtestamentizing" the Psalms

Jesus said, "I have not come to abolish the law, but to fulfill it" (Matt. 5). With these words He boldly proclaimed a new set of guidelines for a new relationship between God and His children was in the works. The Author of the old way had found fault with it and become frustrated with sinful people who were so completely unable to live under the law He'd literally given up caring for them. For the God of love this was unacceptable, and He had a plan to restore what had been lost. He sent His Son to bring heaven to earth and His Spirit to indwell our hearts, and we now live under a New Covenant and in a new kingdom. Grace has fulfilled the old letter of the law by giving us new life in the Spirit, fleshly battles have become spiritual ones, and the way warfare is viewed has changed forever.

It is because of this transformation we now view God, others, and the world in an entirely different way. Praying Today's Psalms evolved out of my personal struggles with the many words in them written under the former covenant that cannot possibly be prayed by those living under the new. God gives us the ability to exchange the hatred for our fellow human beings displayed in the Psalms with love for them, focusing the hatred elsewhere. Combining the old and new, we can also witness the self-reliance we see in the Psalms transformed into reliance upon the indwelling life of the Spirit, along with many other changed paradigms.

The question then becomes if the Psalms are so outdated from a covenantal perspective, why continue to pray them? Simple: the credits far outweigh the debits, and the debits can be transformed into credits. How do we do that? I have used the Psalms as the guiding template while inserting New Testament scriptures and ideals where Old Covenant ones simply won't do. The specific changes, and reasons for those changes, are found in the chapters following the devotional entries.

At the same time, I have taken great care to maintain the integrity of the originals. It is with a profound fear of the Lord I do this, knowing that once you start altering Scripture, even for a good cause, you tread upon thin ice indeed. It is also with the reader's understanding that these devotionals are not meant to be Scripture, but rather a template to aid them in their prayer life, that I do this. It is still today of tremendous beneficial pursuit to anyone to read the Old Testament within the context of its historical and spiritual intent. Yet, if we want to pray them something like this is a good way to be able to.

Layout and Design

Praying Today's Psalms has been published as a set of four devotionals in a series. They have been categorized under the acrostic: P-R-A-Y [Praise, Renewal, Application, and Yearning]. There is an **index** in the front of the daily entries in each devotional, listing the entries by the Psalm number and sub-title located at the top of each one. This will hopefully help narrow your search for a Psalm that fits your particular circumstance at a given time.

The P-R-A-Y acrostic divides the four categories by mood, a brief description of which is as follows:

- Praise: The heart of God for man's worship. Praise is the ultimate gift to give to God. It is the return of His many gifts to us back to Him in worship. Here, the Psalms being both prayers and songs are a perfect fit, because they are both the best means to worship a holy and majestic God just for who He is.

- Renewal: The heart of God for man's transformation. Paul said, "Be transformed by the renewal of your mind" (Rom. 12), and it is in the battleground of the mind the struggle to enter God's kingdom must be fought and won. Renewal is critical to our survival as believers, for if we are to be "new creatures" the old must die and the life of Christ within must be constantly and passionately renewed in His Spirit.

- Application: The heart of God for man's sanctification. Application is engaging in the practice of our faith. It is the process transforming our learning into fruit, and it involves personal disciplines and stepping out in faith to engage in hands-on, lay-down-our-lives mission. It is following the One who led us by example and who commanded us to follow Him in acting out our faith in this world. Application of spiritual truths is absolutely vital to our maturity and to entering God's kingdom. While salvation gives us life eternal and is granted through God's sole proprietorship, sanctification is a life-long process in which we must share in the responsibilities of a partnership with Him.

- Yearning: The heart of God for man's passion. Yearning is the overwhelming desire to find God's presence in the midst of our every circumstance. God and His kingdom are to be diligently and passionately pursued [yearned for] on a daily basis "as the deer pants for water." It is the crying out of man's spirit to God's as the fount of life to a thirsty soul, the cradle of mercy, the smell of victory in the midst of the battle, peace in the midst of confusion, and comfort in the midst of suffering. Yearning brings supernatural hope within the deepest recesses of what the Bible calls our inner man to any situation, no matter how desperate it may seem.

Finally, may I make a couple of suggestions as you go through this devotional:

- You read the chapters following the devotional entries as you proceed. They will give you a much greater understanding of the power and purpose of what praying the Psalms can mean.
- You start a journal to go along with this devotional so you can add your personal revelations and record the sound of His voice as you engage with the Psalmists. It can only serve to help.

Psalms of Yearning
(The heart of God for man's spirit)

The honesty is disturbing, and the songs of lament don't always end with a happy Hallmark-Card-Precious-Moment cliché to try to fix the pain."[1]

"Many of the Psalms are laments or "groans." Our most honest prayers, the deepest sort of cries, are our most desperate ones. When the cries of our minds fail us, we must groan with the Spirit Himself, and those are the most real. It is then that we come to the end of ourselves, and begin to pray according to the will of God."[2]

"Be yourself before God and present Him with your problems—the very things that have brought you to your wits' end."[3]

---

[1] Brian D. McLaren, Open Letter to Songwriters

[2] Michael Wolff

[3] My Utmost for His Highest, ©1992, Discovery House, no pg.

Index of Yearning subtitles

1 - Choosing our friends wisely

5 - In the morning pray and eagerly watch

6 - Rescued from the valley

10 - Frustrations mount as the evil prosper

13 - Life in the Pruner's hands

Poem: *May I See Eternity*

14 - Not one good-no not one

22 - (1-22) - As life hangs in the balance

25 - (1-7, 15-22) - Remembering us for His goodness' sake

27 - Seek the one thing and do not fear

31 - (6-18) - In great distress and grief

35 - Don't let the evil one steal your peace

38 - When sin wastes us, God helps us

39 - Sometimes He silences us

40 - (10-17) - Compassion when it counts

42 - Don't look back-hope in God

Poem: *Where is Your God?*

44 - Never forgetting God through trials
55 - (12-23) - Betrayal of the Wolves
60 - Times when He needs to break us
62 - Wait, and do not be greatly shaken
63 - My soul thirsts and spirit yearns for You
70 - The blessed affliction of the disciple
74 - The enemy tears down our signposts
77 - Remembering God through fearful nights
82 - Arise and judge for the meek
83 - God's vengeance-our obedience
84 - Longing and yearning for His courts
86 - He is good and ready to forgive
88 - In remembrance of the crucified Christ
89 - The lament of loneliness
Poem: *Though He Slay Me*
102 - (1-18) - He is gracious to the distressed
109 - (1-20) - A prayer for protection
109 - (12-31) – Persevering through trials
116 - Return to your rest, O my soul
Poem: *Return to Your Rest*
119 - (17-32) - His words our counselors
119 - (33-48) - The answer for those who question
119 - (81-96) - The consummation of all

perfection

119 - (120-131) - Light to the simple

119 - (145-165) - Revived by His word

119 - (166-176) - Never forgetting His commandments

123 - A sinner's prayer for mercy

130 - He does not mark our iniquities

131 - Finding peace in simplicity

132 - No sleep until His temple is prepared

137 - Worshipping in the midst of defeat

139 - (13-24) - Search me and know my ways

140 - Cover my head in the day of battle

141 - Listening to righteous reproof

142 - Pour out your complaint to God

Poem: *The Prophet's Lot*

1

Choosing our friends wisely

Pray... How blessed, O God, is the man who refuses to let wicked men influence him, or practice sin as those who do not know You, or be counted among those who mock Your truths. Let my delight be forever in your kingdom, Your Word, and Your presence. Lead me to pray without ceasing, meditate upon your truths, and listen to Your voice. Make me like a tree firmly planted in the stream of Your living water. May I not be like the wicked, nor the double-minded man who is unstable in all his ways. Let me not be deceived into thinking bad company won't corrupt good morals, for the wicked will not stand in the time of their judgment, nor shall those who practice evil dwell in the fellowship of the righteous. You know and keep the way of those You have made righteous, having predestined them to adoption as sons. But to the wicked who are destined to perish You will say, "Depart from Me, for I never knew you."

Consider... *Remember those who led you, and who spoke the word of God to you. Considering the result of their conduct, imitate their faith.* The Psalmists waste no time entering the battle no disciple of Christ can escape: our fight to the death between good and evil. Here victory or defeat comes down to relationship which leads to daily spiritual practices, choosing wisely those to whom we listen and emulating those whom we respect. Engaging in fellowship with mentors we can confide in, imitate the conduct of, and count on for sound spiritual advice keeps us on the righteous side of the fight. Today's fellowship has become largely teacher-student versus mentor-apprentice based, with too much emphasis on what we know and too little on what should be the evidence of that: how we live. Disciples are made through a balanced example of learning *and* doing they see in their mentors, not in classrooms. This was Christ's way, but there are so few mentors worthy of doing what He did today. "The fields are white, but the laborers are few." The church is aching for true disciples to bring her out of her malaise. Find, or become, a mentor who leads people from theory into practice, for there is no substitute for this if the Great Commission is our goal.

5

In the morning pray and eagerly watch

Pray... Hear my prayer, Lord, and consider the groanings of my spirit too deep for words. Heed my cries for help, my King and my God, for to You I pour out the longings of my soul! In the morning, I know You hear my voice—in the morning I can offer my prayers and petitions to You and then eagerly watch. But as for the desires of the wicked, You take no pleasure in them. Evil ones cannot dwell in Your presence and the boastful shall not stand in Your glory. You rebuke all who practice sin and lawlessness, and You humble those whose words deceive their brothers. You abide far from those who tempt and mislead.

And yet, by Your great mercy, You have purchased my entrance into the kingdom of Your beloved Son. In Your abiding presence, O God, I bow in reverence for apart from Your sacrifice I would be lost and apart you're your Spirit my foe would be too strong for me. Lead me in Your righteous ways and make the path straight and clear before me, for there is nothing reliable in what the enemy whispers in my ear. His spirit is deception itself and his tongue is a beckoning grave, yet at times I allow him to cater to my former desires. Oh, get thee behind me, Satan! Find him guilty in Your courts, O God! Turn his evil plans against him and make him as nothing to me. Rebuke and cast this liar out, for his rebellion never rests and he causes Your sons to stray from Your holy ways. He hardens their hearts, so they do not fear You nor walk in obedience to Your commands. Let me remember well from where I came, Lord, and take refuge in You, reawakening gladness and forever singing a joyful song! Yes, those who love You dwell in Your presence and forever exalt in Your kingdom. It is You who blesses the righteous man, Lord Jesus, as with a shield of fine armor You surround him with favor.

Consider... *And in the early morning...He arose and went out and departed to a lonely place and was praying there.* There is something special about spending time with God in the morning. Our enemy arises early to deceive and defeat us with the falsehoods he whispers in our ears. He lures us into battle the moment we awaken from sleep and continues to engage us until we lay down. We are fresh and alert in the morning, before Satan and his minions have gained a foothold. It stands to reason then that morning is the best time to come into God's courts, seek His counsel, and plan for our day. We can either get our marching orders from our commander before the battle begins or require crisis management and intensive care after we've sustained injuries. In the morning order your prayer to God and eagerly watch. David, the man after God's own heart and Jesus, the man who was God, did so. Start the day with good news, wisdom, and a battle-plan from on high before the enemy presses in and be surrounded with the shield of God's favor as you go out to face the day!

6
Rescued from the valley

Pray... Sometimes You need to discipline me for my good that I may share in Your holiness, O God. Be gracious to me when my endurance falters and restore me in a spirit of gentleness. Heal me, Lord Jesus, if I become dismayed and confused in the depths of my inner man. How long, O Lord? How often shall I feel the prick of the thorns that distance us? When will You transform my thoughts and grant deliverance and freedom from sin? Save me in Your tender mercies, for I hear no mention of You in this valley of shadows. Only You can raise me up from this darkness in thanksgiving and praise. It seems such a distant hope at times, for I become weary with my sighing and numb as I wait. At night my bed hears the sighs and by day my mind is overcome with despair, for hope deferred makes my heart sick. My faith is shaken as anxiety and grief endure and my strength wanes as the battle presses in.

Depart from me, Satan! Leave me now, O evil one who tempts and oppresses me with sinful desires. Away with you, for you live to deceive and to accuse me day and night before the throne of my God! Get thee behind me, for the Lord Jesus has heard the voice of my sobs and come down from His throne to purchase me from the grave. Through my trials, my Good Shepherd has heard my cries, and I know He receives my prayer. Soon you shall be the one stricken and dismayed! Yes, You shall be turned back and surely and suddenly defeated.

Consider... *Be anxious for nothing, but in everything by prayer and supplication with thanksgiving let your requests be made known to God. And the peace of God, which surpasses all comprehension, shall guard your hearts and your minds in Christ Jesus.* Even the most faithful of God's children find themselves plagued with seasons of doubt. They can come as a result of Satan's scheming, self-inflicted wounds, or God's testing. There is nothing more unsettling than feeling we have lost touch with the Spirit within, especially when the reasons why seem to escape us. When we have experienced God's kingdom on earth life without feeling it becomes a twilight zone where we don't belong in heaven or on earth. We grow weary and numb, feeling like we're a burden to both God and man. Our spirit cries out, "How long, O Lord?!" But regardless of what our feelings are telling us, we must press on through the darkness. In the midst of your tears, you must find it within yourself to remember all the times He has raised you from faithlessness and given you a new beginning. Look back and remember, then look forward with renewed faith. In Christ we have the power to say, "Depart from me O doer of iniquity, for my God has heard the voice of my weeping!" In Christ Jesus we can press on to the light that in due season always shines through! Our patient endurance is the way to the perfection He seeks for us. It comes through just putting one foot of faith in front of the last one. It may not feel good, but it is good.

10
The nature of the beast

Pray... Why does it seem You are distant to me at times, O Lord? Why do I not hear Your voice or sense Your presence? The wicked one, whose nature it is to accuse, loves to taunt me at those times, but You can silence his voice and defeat his plans for me. His children boast of their heart's desires and greedy men who follow him curse and spurn You. Because of the pride that dwells within their souls, they reject You. Believing there is no God, they seek only worldly gain in all they do. They are blind to Your truth, O Lord, for it is spiritually discerned and out of their reach. Mocking their adversaries, evil men do as their master does, thinking they shall never be moved from their positions of power, nor shall they see adversity. Their mouths are full of curses, deceit, and oppression, and their tongues are a fire full of deadly poison, mischief, and wickedness. Their master abides in shadows, as from his hiding place he prays upon the innocent. His eyes watch in stealth for the unfortunate and naïve, as he crouches like a lion waiting to pounce. He lurks in shadows ready to catch the afflicted and draw them into his net. He springs his traps, and the ignorant and unbelieving give in to his deceptions. He thinks You have forgotten, and that his wicked deeds and acts are hidden from Your sight.

I pray arise, O Lord! O my Lord and King, lift up Your righteous right hand, for You do not forsake the afflicted and You will not forget me! Surely You see all and have beheld the mischief and chaos Satan and his minions have caused and have weighed everything upon Your scales. The lowly and the poor in spirit commit themselves to You, for You are the helper of the orphan and the widow. I pray, break Satan's spell of evil! Seek out and defeat his wickedness until it torments no more! Earthly kingdoms may rise and fall but You, Lord Jesus, are King forever and ever. You have heard the desires of the humble and will strengthen their hearts. Vindicate the faithful who are oppressed, that the deceptions of the evil one may triumph no more. Above all, O God, grant me the peace of Your kingdom, knowing vengeance is Yours and I am, as a son of God, to be a peacemaker.

Consider... *In addition to all, taking up the shield of faith with which you will be able to extinguish all the flaming arrows of the evil one.* Most churchgoers are woefully unprepared to cross swords with our sworn enemy. Praying the Psalms, like no other method available, can make the believer aware of, and prepared for, just how evil, cunning, resourceful, and tenacious Satan is. The conflicts David speaks of so often with his worldly foes paint a perfect tapestry of ours with our unworldly foes. And make no mistake, he is absolutely, resolutely, and shamelessly dedicated to your destruction. Their master cannot be shamed into ceasing his attacks no matter how many times he is defeated, he will just use his defeat to cater to your pride. He is the master of chaos, leading you into confusion, the master of catastrophe, leading you into fear, and the master of false provision, leading you into Laodicean lukewarmth and numbness. And it is the subtlety of the enemy, leading us like frogs in the proverbial hot water to that Laodicean state (Rev. 3) that has most in its grasp. The Psalms can reawaken anyone to the players and the battle involved and keep them aware that the battle never ends. So, get on your knees and fight like a man. Keep yourself firmly in the shadow of the One in whom even the Devil believes, and shudders!

13
Life in the Pruner's hands

Pray... How long, O Lord, will I go on feeling this distance between us? How long will this feeling You have hidden Your face from me endure? Shall I take lonely counsel within my soul while my heart feels the numbness as  the shadows grow? Shall I go on, day after day, harboring these questions in my heart? How long will You allow the enemy to mock as the weight of anxiety and temptation are so heavily upon me?

Hear my prayer, Lord Jesus. Consider my desperate state and answer me, O Lord my God! Be the light in me that overcomes the darkness and chases the shadows of doubt away. Be my abiding hope that makes the hopelessness flee, lest the numbness continue, my enemy win the day, and I give him good reason to boast. Don't let Satan rejoice in times of confusion, as I stand before You with my trust shaken. How I long to feel Your abiding presence, Your tender mercies, and rejoice in the steadfast love again! How I desire to know the peace of standing in Your righteousness and Your kingdom once more. Forgetting what lays behind me and reaching forward to what lays ahead, let me press on again toward the goal for the prize of Your upward calling! Oh, when will my heart sing to You once again, knowing You have dealt graciously with me?

Consider... *So do not despise the discipline of the Almighty, for He inflicts pain and gives relief—He wounds, and His hands also heal.* It is hard to embrace the kind of despair that comes when we feel like God has turned away from us. We feel alone, lost, and without divine counsel. Yet it is those who have experienced this sort of spiritual drought and endured in faith who come to know God more fully. There is not a true kingdom saint who fails to understand that His loving Savior sometimes inflicts pain and suffering, for through enduring trials from many sources true disciples are birthed. To know Jesus is to know all of Him, not just His comforts. If the Father was pleased to crush Him at the Cross of Calvary, can we who have been entrusted with the furtherance of His kingdom on earth expect anything less? Wounding and healing are God's patient path to sanctification for His chosen ones. "Through many tribulations we *must* enter the kingdom of God. Do all to find it in your battered and doubting soul at times like this to praise the pruner, convinced that nothing shall separate you from the love His pruning brings to bear upon you. Learn in every trial to count it all joy as you endure, knowing that only in the kiln does the unfinished pottery become shining, perfect, and complete, lacking in nothing. This is God's power perfected in our weakness.

A Poem: May I See Eternity

Through all my sins and all of Satan's tempt's,
all of my fears and all my laments
Through all the trials I must endure to be
Perfect, complete, lacking in nothing—
my eternity secured
Yes, through it all may it be said of me
"He saw through the day into eternity"
For the evil one seeks only to kill and
destroy my vision of my heavenly home
To supplant with worries of the day,
my sight of unearthly thrones
And with anxieties aplenty over
that temporal and closely viewed
Keeps my eyes of faith from
moment to moment arising renewed
Keeping me concerned about
such a great many things
And from the important part, Jesus,
just sitting at Your feet
To make me grumble, to complain, and to say
"I can take no more," my faith in You to betray
To cloud what should be abundantly clear
And to cast aside what is forever for that which is here
Evil knows if it can obscure
eternal life for a bowl of its Pottage today
It will steal my heritage though I later seek it with tears
My eternal home to bargain away for a paltry few years
If it can just abide fully in my face,
to cloud my sight and obscure my view of grace
If I cannot see the forest for the trees,
the honey for the swarming bees
The ocean for the crashing waves,
anxiety's victory will be sure

And will have found the fool it so craves
If it can but make me forget
To on the day's elementary affairs of men my eyes set
If fear's cry can cause me to from the plow look back
Shrinking from the battle, and succumbed to its attacks
But to set mind and heart above,
where my Lord Christ is seated
Should be the sum of my desire, more than ever I needed
And more than all hopes behind or preceded, the spirit at
peace, the flesh utterly defeated,
shaping the future of who I am to be
O God, let me see through the clouds of evil,
anxiety, and fear held 'fore me this day
To catch but a glimpse of eternity

14
No one good—no, not one

Pray... The fool believes in his heart You don't exist, O God. Yet, as I try to follow You even I, who does believe, falls short of Your holiness. I think sinful thoughts and commit sinful deeds. There is no one without sin—no one whose flesh is pure. You look down from heaven upon the children You have created, to see if there are any who truly understand and seek after You. But we all stumble at times, giving in to the lusts of our flesh, our eyes, our pride, and our worldly desires. There is no one righteous in the flesh—no, not even one. I thank You that our perfection is in spirit and not flesh, and that You continue to perfect us in the faith.

I, the one who wishes to do good, at times do the very thing I hate. I, the one who is willing, at times do not do what I wish. I, the spiritual man, have this body of death in my flesh where sin dwells. But You have set me free from it and shown me it is not I who does wrong but this tormentor in my flesh. Therefore, there is now no condemnation for me because I am in Your Son, Christ Jesus! Help me to look to You and fear, O God, for You are with the righteous who revere You and call upon Your name. Without Your Spirit guiding me, I would be unrepentant, practice sin, and ignore conviction and counsel. Lord Jesus, You are the hope and strength of the needy. Impart Your righteousness to me, and let Your abiding presence fill my heart, the temple of Your Spirit. O Lord, forgive my sin and blot out my iniquity!

Restore me from my captivity to the law of sin and death in the flesh, remind me of my true identity in Christ, and set me free to live life in the Spirit! Then I will rejoice, and Your kingdom will be exalted!

Consider... *So now, no longer am I the one doing it, but sin which dwells in me.* Romans 7 is often misinterpreted to justify sin and to perpetuate the lie that we are just sinners in need of grace if we are to survive at all. No less than three times in this passage Paul says, "It is not I [the spiritual man, the true me] sinning but an unwanted tormentor that lives in my flesh." And consider this, if Paul was indeed just a sinner why, after providing an extensive list of all the things that would condemn him in Romans 7, does he open Romans 8 with, "There is no condemnation for those in Christ Jesus—for him?" We need to admit we all have the same tormentor, but rather than focusing on that seek to find where Christ is alive in us and operate from there. That is where we will find no provision for the flesh, and where we will find our passion and heart for our righteous mission in life. This is why Paul exhorts us, in that same letter to the Romans, to walk in the Spirit so we won't carry out the deeds of the tormentor. Paul's "I myself" was a spiritual righteous man and not a sinner.

22 *(1-22)*
As life hangs in the balance

Pray... My God, my God, why does it feel at times You have forsaken me? Why does it seem You stand distant and aloof from my trials? Why does it seem Your ears are deaf to the groanings of my spirit and the requests of my prayers? I cry out by day but get no answers. I plead by night—I have not been silent. I know You are holy and sit enthroned upon the praise of Your people. There is no one else I can turn to, for You are trustworthy and the only One who can deliver. I have cried out to You before and been rescued—You did not stand afar off but rewarded my faith. Yet now I feel like something less than Your child. I am mocked by the tormentor of my soul as he exploits my fears. Into my discouragement He whispers, "So you trust in the Lord, then let Him rescue you. Let the God who delights in you deliver you."

I know You fashioned me, brought me from the womb, and gave me reason to trust in You from the beginning to stand amazed by Your creation! I have seen and acknowledged Your existence, so do not remain distant for trouble is near and there is no other redeemer but You! Many temptations surround me Lord. Deceptions of the wicked one encircle me! The evil one roars with a desire to tear me apart as hapless prey. I am poured out like water and all my thoughts are confused. My heart feels heavy as wax and my strength fails me. My endurance wanes and I am questioning my resolve to fight on. I sit motionless in the dust of doubt and fear as the forces of hell press in, encircling me and piercing my mind and my heart! I try in vain to count my blessings as my tormentor looks on, gloating, and asks, "Has God said?" He tempts me with the lusts of forbidden fruit. Please, Lord, do not remain afar off! O my strength, come quickly to help me and deliver my life from the failings of my flesh! Let me be found precious in Your sight and save me from the power of the forces arrayed against me! Rescue me from the mouth of the prowling Lion. Give me reason to declare anew Your name to my brothers, stating boldly, "Greater is He who is in me!" In the midst of the fellowship, let me arise from the ashes once more to follow and worship You.

Consider... *Beloved, do not be surprised at the fiery ordeal among you which comes upon you for your testing, as though some strange thing were happening to you.* This portrait of Christ's crucifixion becomes a painfully real picture of our own circumstances at times. If we are to share in His sufferings we must be crucified upon the crosses of trial from above, attack from beneath, and weakness from within. Jesus didn't try to hide His anguish and pain from His Father, so why should we? "Through many tribulations we must enter the kingdom of God." Christ's relationship with the Father was a union built upon absolute integrity, no covering up or superficiality involved. Jesus asked the Father to grant this same relationship between Himself and us when He prayed, "I have given them the glory that You gave me, that they may be one as We are one—I in them and You in Me." Don't mask the pain the One who searches the heart knows full-well is there. Honesty in the trials, like praise in the victories, is all a part of being *one*. That's the integrity that is critical as life for the saint sometimes hangs in the balance.

25 (1-7, 15-22)
Remembering us for His goodness' sake

Pray... To You, Lord, I lift up my soul. Lord Jesus, let me trust in You, the One who lives to make intercession for me, and not be ashamed by the lies of my accuser the Devil. I pray, don't allow this heartless foe to win the day. May no one who waits upon You be ashamed, but rather let the deceivers, the treacherous ones, and their master be the ones defeated. Grant me revelation of Your ways, O Lord, and walk me down Your righteous path. As I look to Your Spirit, lead me in Your truth and teach me, for He is the Counselor You sent to fill and empower me. Remember Your everlasting covenant, my Savior—the promise of Your tender mercy and love that endures forever. Do not hold the sins and the weaknesses of my flesh against me, nor call to memory the day's transgressions, but remember Your covenant and forgive. For Your goodness' sake have mercy upon me.

Draw my eyes always toward You, for You alone can pluck my feet out of the jaws of the trap the enemy has waiting. Turn to me and have mercy on me for I feel emptied and weary. The troubles of my heart have increased for hope deferred makes the heart sick. Therefore, bring me out of this place, pour grace upon my wound, and forgive. Do not ignore my enemy and his minions who stand with him against me. He hates me with an everlasting and cruel hatred, so I pray bring my wind-tossed soul into Your harbor and deliver me from the squall. Despising the shame of the enemy, let me put my trust fully in You. Let the integrity and uprightness of Your presence preserve me as I wait for

You. And not just me, O Lord, redeem Your church from her many troubles.

Consider...

Yet God does not take away life but plans ways so that the banished one may not be cast out from Him. When the troubles of our heart enlarge, and our thinned-by-sin wineskin threatens to burst because of the life of the new wine within, we can always repent, change our course, and call upon God's power to renew us. Those in Christ need never again be counted among people who have no hope. The believer's assurance is that God always remembers us for *His* goodness' sake. But do we return His kindness? Is our image of God in times of trial likewise remembered by us for His goodness? Do we look upon our circumstances in faith, so that we don't keep Him at a distance? Or in times when we don't feel His presence, do we make Him into a likeness of something He is not? We can never let current circumstances, for good or bad, tarnish our vision of eternal outcomes. No matter the predicaments, we must not allow them to create in our mind's eye a lesser vision of our heavenly Redeemer. We must remember Him as He faithfully remembers us: for goodness' sake. And that's a good thing, because nothing good dwells in us apart from who He is and what He has indwelt in us.

27

Seek the one thing and do not fear

Pray... Lord, You are my light and the One who calls and then leads me. Whom shall I fear? Your strength and life abide in me, and of whom shall I be afraid? Satan seeks to lure me with the temptations of my flesh, confronting me with shame, doubt, and fear. But as long as I walk by faith, considering myself dead to sin and alive unto You, Yours will be the victory. Though his armies may arise against me, and he win some battles, my heart need not fear. When the powers of darkness bring the fight to me, I can endure by placing my trust in You and pressing on. One thing I have desired of You, and that I seek diligently: to abide in Your presence and walk in Your kingdom all the days of my life. Oh God, let me behold Your beauty as I come in prayer before Your throne! In times of trouble, You hide me in Your love—yes, in the secret place of grace You secure me. You set me high upon a rock and lift my eyes above every trouble that surrounds me, that my spirit might embrace You fully. Let me offer sacrifices of joy in Your presence, O God, and sing praises to Your name! Hear as I cry out to You, speak to my spirit and restore me to Your kingdom!

When You say to me, "Seek My face," may the cry of my heart be, "Your face, Lord Jesus, I shall seek." Do not let me wander in search of You, nor turn me away in righteous anger, for You alone are my light and my comfort. O God of my salvation, You have promised You will not leave me nor forsake me and that nothing shall snatch me out of Your hand. When all around me turn away, and the enemy demands to sift me like wheat, You are there to care for my soul. Because of the temptations of darkness, teach me Your way, O Lord, and lead me on the narrow path. Do not allow me to be delivered to Satan's will, for he speaks falsehoods in my ear and deceives with his every word. I would have lost heart long ago had I not believed that I would witness Your goodness in the land of the living! Wait upon the Lord, O my soul—be of good courage and He will strengthen you. Surely, He will help you. Surely, He will uphold you with His righteous right hand. Oh yes, I say, wait upon the Lord!

Consider... *Seek first His kingdom and His righteousness, and all these things shall be added unto you.* There is no enemy too strong, no temptation too seductive, no valley too expansive nor no task too great when the one thing we seek is the very real kingdom of heaven on earth. Consider the above verse with Jesus' most famous prayer, the first request of which is, "Thy kingdom come, Thy will be done *on earth as it is in heaven.*" Do you see it? In both passages the kingdom comes first and everything else follows. We must, as Paul says, "Press on" to the upward calling, the highest of which is what God chose to be the announcement of Jesus' coming: "Repent, for the kingdom of heaven is at hand!" We must lay aside all else and remember the one thing: seeking first His kingdom by continuing on in the journey of enduring faith. So stop seeking all else and seek the first thing. Then you will surely see His goodness in the land of the living: that "better country" Hebrews speaks of. We need not wait to get to heaven to see it, for Jesus brought it and it's never left us.

31 *(6-18)*
In great distress and grief

Pray... Lord, help me shun the possessions and idols of man, and trust only in You. Let me be glad and rejoice in Your faithfulness and mercy. Give me faith to believe You have considered my troubles, You are watching over me in times of adversity, and You will not abandon me to the plans of my enemy. I pray set my feet in a place of peace through Your grace extended to me, for my soul is troubled, my vision fades in the shadows, and my faith is being taxed by the war that rages between flesh and spirit. My nights are spent in worry and my days are consumed with sighing. Sometimes I am defeated by sin, my will to fight on wanes, a life full of promise seems to waste away and hope suffers. Both friend and stranger doubt me, and Satan's attacks bring about doubt and fear. The forces of lawlessness increase, and my heart seems to grow cold. I am rejected and those I wished would embrace me avoid me instead. I am forgotten like a dead man or mocked as one who has lost his mind. I become like an empty and broken vessel, listening to the slander and the lies. Satan counsels against me, scheming to gain victory over my faith and rob me of a life rooted and alive in You. Therefore, anxiety and defeat encircle me.

Nevertheless, Lord, my heart's desire remains: to live fully and only for You. I cry out, "Bring me back into Your kingdom of justice, righteousness, and peace!" My spirit proclaims, "You are my God and my times are in Your hand. Deliver me from the clutches of doubt, temptation, and darkness! Make Your face to shine upon me once again, and again let me feel the warmth of Your presence!" Renew me for Your mercies' sake, O Lord. Do not let the shame of sin overwhelm me, but rather let me hold fast to Your promises and remember who I am in Christ. Confound the worldly forces of this darkness! Silence them and send them scurrying back to the depths from which they came. Let their lying lips that speak insolent things against You and Your righteous ones, so proudly and with such contempt, be struck dumb and mute. Deliver me, I pray, O my God, and send them back into the pit from which they came.

Consider... *Therefore, I will not restrain my mouth. I will speak in the anguish of my spirit. I will complain in the bitterness of my soul.* Let's not candy-coat this, there are times when the schemes of the enemy, the battle with our flesh, and the seeming distance of God cast our lives into a desperate whirlpool of confusion and despair. We spend our days in the fog of doubt while Satan's plans seem to charge on un-opposed. The flesh and the spirit are at war, and we seem more helpless spectators than able combatants. There are two truths we must hold on to now: first, our battle is not against flesh and blood but against evil itself. It is not the circumstances or the people, but rather the powers behind them we must understand and endure. Second, He will not always give us victory, for it is in the process of enduring we find perfection. We must start each day hearing Paul's ex-hortation to forget what lays behind us, both the good and bad, and press on towards God's upward calling! We serve a King and kingdom not of this world, so take the fight to the heavenly battlefield and cry out to your heavenly Comrade in Arms in the anguish of your spirit! Paul summarized his life at the end by proclaiming, "I have fought the good fight. I have finished the race. I have kept the faith!" Doesn't sound like a bed of roses, this journey.

35(19-28)
Not letting the evil one steal our peace

Pray... Lord, don't let evil rejoice over me. Keep Satan, the evil one full of perversity who hates me, from being justified in mocking me. He is not for peace but devises deceitful plans against me as I seek the peace of Your kingdom. He opens his mouth wide against me and taunts, "Aha, aha! My eyes have seen the darkness in you even as you seek the light!" This You have seen, O Lord, for nothing escapes Your notice.

Therefore, draw near to me now for apart from You I am defenseless and can do nothing. Arouse Yourself! Awaken to my side, my vindication, and my cause, O my God and my Lord! Vindicate me in Your righteousness, for any righteousness of my own is like filthy rags to You. Let not evil rejoice over me, nor the flesh overcome me. Don't let Satan say in his heart, "Ah, so I would have the victory for he is mine! He has removed his hand from the plow and I have caused him to shrink back to destruction." Rather Lord, confound and utterly defeat this one who rejoices in my trial. Clothe him who lifts himself up against me with dishonor, even as those who favor my righteous cause are glad! Let them say continually, "The Lord Jesus, Lord of heaven and earth upon whose shoulders our government rests, be magnified because He takes pleasure in the triumphs of His servants." May my brothers bear witness and say, "O evil, where is your victory? O darkness, where is your sting?" Then my tongue shall declare Your goodness, offering praise in the day of Your triumph!

Consider...*And His name will be called...Prince of Peace. There will be no end to the increase of His government or of peace.* The evil one knows if he can steal our peace he can keep us from the kingdom, for peace is the cornerstone of the kingdom of heaven one earth. Nothing is broken in the kingdom, for all things there are in God's capable hands. Only in the kingdom of man, where our enemy wreaks constant fear and chaos, will you find anything to fret about. Therefore, when the powers of darkness throw obstacles to peace in our way we can simply remind ourselves which kingdom we are of and find it once more. "The mind set on the Spirit is life and peace." Faith and peace go hand in hand. To live in the kingdom means trusting the assurance of things [spiritual] *not seen*, over that seen which Satan puts in our path to make us anxious [fleshly]. Don't give the devil opportunity to say, "Aha, I have my desire, for I have pulled him into my kingdom and swallowed him up in stress and anxiousness." Rather, see to it He is confounded when he cannot steal your peace because you have made the choice to be a kingdom citizen. Jesus, King of your kingdom, rules in justice and righteousness forever (Isa. 9:6-7) and will guard your heart and mind. Through the Spirit, He will give you peace the world and its ruler-of-flesh could never steal. It's all a matter of which kingdom you elect.

38

When sin wastes us, God helps us

Pray... As You train me up in righteousness, O God, Your admonitions and corrections test my endurance. Your convictions can cut deeply, Your words can shake my soul, and Your might and power can make me fear and tremble. I feel the double-edged sword of Your pruning power cutting deeply into me, dividing soul and spirit, making me grieve over the sin that lives in my members. At times iniquities rise over my head, and like a heavy burden they are too weighty for me. My wounds become foul and festering from the battle that rages within. I am troubled and humiliated, and I feel anxiety and the burden of my error. I feel the fever of Your conviction, and there is no soundness in my soul. I become feeble and undone, groaning and grieving due to choices I make to follow the desires of my flesh.

My heart pants, my strength fails me, and the light of my eyes grows dim. My loved ones and friends fail to understand my affliction. The evil one lays his snares for me. Seeking only my harm he constantly strategizes for my destruction. He devises deceptions to undo me and yet I, like a deaf man, must not listen. I, like a mute man, must not engage him in reply. I must be like one who does not hear, and in whose mouth is no response before this tormentor of my soul. But Lord, my true desire is before You and my sighing is not hidden from You. Let me look to the heavens and hope in and raise my voice to You! I know you will hear my cries and be my advocate in the face of his constant accusations. If You did not respond, delivering me from this body of death, the sin You came to defeat would win the day. As my feet slipped, transgression would claim its prize, and as I succumbed and was carried by its tide, darkness would rejoice. What was supposed to have died would defeat me, strengthening my enemy. He would multiply his attacks, exchanging evil for the good I try to do. He swears to my destruction because I follow You and try to do what is good and right. So let me confess, with a repentance without regret that leads me to avenge sin for righteousness' sake and stand fast in Your kingdom! I pray, come near me quickly to help me, O defender of my soul and God of my salvation!

Consider... *And because lawlessness is increased, most people's love will grow cold.* We've all listened to the lies of Satan and, because of the sin in our flesh, fallen headlong, willfully and knowingly into his traps. While the consequences are great for denying the depths of sin to which we can fall, the destruction will increase greatly if we cover it up and rationalize it. If we continue on that path, we can become numb to the sin and it becomes a practice rather than a stumble. This eventually leads us into the damning condition the Bible calls lawlessness, a place where we no longer feel the need for repentance because we've ignored it for so long. No matter how many times we have succumbed, we must never stop acknowledging our failings, repenting, and confessing to both God and man. We must return to our daily place of quiet with Him, even if we have to crawl to get there. We must bring forth fruits of repentance and strive to reawaken our first love, no matter how futile it may seem at times. We will find always that the depths of His mercies will exceed the depths of our sin if we will but endure through refusing to give in to iniquity.

39
Sometimes He silences us

Pray... Lord, let me guard my ways lest I sin with my tongue. As evil and flesh taunt me, calm my soul, silence my mouth, and grant me peace and restraint. As a lamb before its shearers is dumb, let me be silent in the midst of the chaos. Keep my mind focused above, where You dwell, and let me not withhold the good desires You have placed in my heart. As I consider their plight, may righteous indignation and love concerning justice for the afflicted and deceived stir within me. Oh yes, let holy fire within my heart burn! Help me to see what awaits and what the measure of my days will be. Remind me of how aware I must remain to the lure of the flesh. Indeed, the time of a man is of no account and the age of a man is as nothing before You. Certainly, every man at his best is short-lived, and in the flesh every man lives on borrowed time. He busies himself in vain as he stores up treasures on earth, where moths eat and rust corrodes, without knowing who will enjoy them.

And now, Lord, what do I wait for? Do I truly put my trust in You? To whom else would I turn, for You speak the words of eternal life to me. Therefore, deliver me from my transgressions and don't allow me to give the foolish cause to mock. When it is You who corrects me remain silent and listen. Let me draw near to You to hear rather than offer the sacrifice of fools. Let reproof, rebuke, correction, and righteousness training come to me, and let conviction from Your Spirit guide me. When You correct and prune me, I feel the sting of Your rod, but I know my sin would shorten my days if You withheld admonishment from me. Oh hear my prayer, Lord Jesus, and give ear to my cry! Remove these doubts that toss me to and fro, that my mind might be renewed for the days left to me on earth. Do not be silent as You bear witness to my sighs, for I am as a stranger here—a sojourner, as were all the faithful who have gone forth before me.

Consider... *Even a fool, when he keeps silent, is considered wise. When he closes his lips he is counted prudent...In repentance and rest you shall be saved. In quietness and trust is your strength.* Even kings of nations get to feeling insignificant when reflecting upon the nature of eternity. When faced with such enormity it is easy to feel small and insignificant. We speak out for God and are mocked, yet when we try to keep silent the fire of Christ's love burns within. Dealing with both a sinful world and our sinful nature leads to mounting frustration, so we cry out, "Give me answers to all of this, O God! Show me the end of it all, and what part I am to play!" Then we are ashamed of our foolish demands, and just want God to look away. We become silent, close our mouths, and begin to listen in quietness to the One who whispers His Rhema word to us. Perspective is regained, and we remember that He ministers through a tranquil and quiet life better than through many words. If we want to show understanding beyond our years, we need to learn the wisdom to know when to be silent and just live before others in such a way that the love and peace of God ruling in our hearts does the talking.

40 (10-17)
Compassion when it counts

Pray... Don't let me hide the truth of Your righteousness and mercy within my heart Lord, for I desire to declare Your kingdom and the joy of salvation to my brothers. Let me proclaim boldly the truth of who You are to the congregation of witnesses surrounding me. Lead me to lay aside every burden, and the sin which so easily entangles, and run with endurance the race You have set before me! I pray, never withhold Your tender mercies but let Your lovingkindness and Your truth continually preserve me. The principalities and powers of darkness seek to surround and oppress me. Their desire is that my sin would overtake me, leaving me ashamed to come into Your presence. At times they know my troubles seem overwhelming, and when they press in my strength can fail me.

Make my deliverance Your pleasure, Lord Jesus! Make haste, O God, to help me in my brokenness. Let evil and all her minions be bound, for they seek to undermine my faith. Cause them to be exposed and cast out, that my eyes might see the deception in their twisted plans. Confound Satan with Your power alive in me and turn the tables on his attempts to gloat over me. Let all those who seek You rejoice and be glad in You, and may all who love Your salvation say continually, "The Lord Jesus Christ be magnified!" Though I be made the fool for Your sake, let others be prudent. Though I be made weak, let them be strong. May they be distinguished even as I am found without honor, and though I be rendered poor and needy, reassure me Your Spirit will always be with me. You are my help and my deliverer, Lord, therefore do not delay. Let Your Spirit be magnified in me, Lord Jesus, that I might continually know the righteousness, justice, and peace of Your kingdom!

Consider...*For we know that the whole creation groans and suffers the pains of childbirth together until now. And not only this, but also we ourselves, having the first fruits of the Spirit, even we ourselves groan within ourselves.*" Even the most devout of believers are subjected to the futility of sin in God's creation. But they bear this "unwillingly" and anxiously await their ultimate redemption by the Son of God. They know their perfecting is found in the kilns of endurance and keep their steadfast faith in a world that seems to have driven them into the darkness and now makes them wait endlessly for the light. The truth is there are no guarantees of success as the world would define it for the disciple. But no matter the personal disappointments that await, there is always an inner joy available through bearing the fruit of God's love and finding the peace of His kingdom on earth. God's kindness saved us from an eternity far worse than any desert He may now cause us to travel through, and the joys available in the race He has given us to run far outweigh the price required to run it. At times He will make haste to help us, and at times He will make us endure tests from above, below, and within. Temporary victories are all the powers of darkness will realize if we remain steadfast. Jesus' compassions, so new every morning, will carry the day for any who will but take up their crosses and follow Him.

42
Don't look back—hope in God

Pray... As the deer pants for brooks of water, so also let my soul yearn for You, O God. May I thirst for You—for the living God. When sadness, shame, fear and doubt are my companions the enemy loves to taunt, asking, "Where now is your God?" I wonder, how long must I endure this sin of unbelief that dwells in me? My desire is to know Your presence and dwell in Your kingdom, and though I long to leave and be with You forever, I know to remain can mean fruitful service for me. When I consider this, my soul becomes anxious within me. Here I am able to go with my brothers into the fellowship, with the voice of joy as we break bread together. But would it not be better to leave my troubles and come be with You?

Why are you cast down, O my soul, and why have you so little peace at times? Hope in God, for you shall yet praise Him for the love you find in His presence. O Jesus, my soul is heavy within me! Remind me, I pray, of Your tender mercies with each breath I take. Deep calls unto deep with the revelation of Your Spirit within me, for it divides bone and marrow. All His waves have broken over me, causing me to cry out, "Why does it seem You have forgotten me? Why do I lose my peace because of the oppression the sin that dwells in my flesh? Why do I seem at times I am bound with chains when You have come to set me free?" With a force meant to break my spirit Satan mocks me. Once more he taunts me asking, "Where now is your God? Has He destined you only to suffer without purpose, and to forever strive without victory?" Oh, why are you cast down my soul, and why are you so full of doubt? Know that your suffering is but for a moment, and your joy will be eternal! Know now that the Lord commands His mercies to be with you in the daytime and His songs in the night! Be anxious for nothing, but seek first His kingdom and His righteousness, and all else shall be abundantly supplied to you. The die is cast, Lord. My hope is in You and that I shall yet live to praise You within the fellowship of saints. You are my ever-present help and the God in Whom I trust. To whom else would I turn?

Consider... *Do not call to mind the former things, nor ponder things of the past. Behold, I will do something new. Now it will spring forth. Will you not be aware of it?* There is a dangerous tendency we believers have when spiritual dryness sets in. During the times of pruning, as God's waves of testing can consume us, we look back to easier or more fruitful times and yearn to return to them. Reflecting for a season to consider His past works, or to examine ourselves at His Table, is beneficial. However, to dwell in the past in an effort to avoid our present reality is to seek to walk by sight and not by faith. We are to live in the now, look forward in faith, and realize our God is *always* doing something new. He is therefore always remaking us to prepare us for it. We must forget what lies behind and press on toward the goal, lest we not be aware of His new direction for us and perhaps miss it entirely. Hope in God, for He has blessings waiting in the future for those who don't try to avoid the now. We will never experience His "new thing" by clinging to the past. He has waiting for us many revelations we shall yet praise Him for, but they'll never appear in our rear-view mirror.

Where is Your God?
Where now are You, O Lord?
My flesh taunts me for an answer,
my soul is cast down within me
"Where now is your God?" the tempter
tempts as my heart melts within me
As a wanderer in a parched and dry wasteland
Longing only for the sound of Your righteous command
Remembering the glories of fellowship with my King
A reason sure hearty praises to sing
But such ancient thoughts now
become reasons only for my tears
Parted from joyous past by suffering's
furrows over the years
Only clouds now these longing eyes to see
Cruel reminders of this present tragedy
Deep calls unto deep at the sound of Your Spirit-wind
Blowing seemingly upon all those You call "friend"
But only waves and billows roll over me as
I hear persistent taunts of mine enemy
"Where now is your God?" as with a breaking of my bones
Reminding me once again of the terrors of feeling so alone
"Command Your graces to me," my spirit cries out in despair
"Command Your song to me, my brokenness to repair!"
A prayer to the God of my life,
a plea to bring quickly end to this strife
A prayer to the God of mine and all creation
To once again be the source of all my elation
Hope in God, O my soul, cling desperately for
I shall yet arise to praise Him
Hope in God, and do not lightly raise Him
Though thorns and thistles, and the sweat of your brow
Seem the sum of your lot, 'tis but a test for you now
To find if the endurance of saints is the
brand upon your heart

For be this trial life's journey, 'tis but eternity's start
That when the enemy asks, "Where now is your Lord?"
Heart, soul, mind, and strength
would awaken in one steadfast accord
And cry, "I shall bear the indignation of my
God until my just cause He pleads
He will execute my justice, knowing fully all my needs"
Oh, do not rejoice over me though I fall,
and at times in darkness plod
For when He brings me out into
His light, and His righteousness I see
Shame will be the clothing of all who taunted,
"Where now is your God?"

44
Never forgetting God through trials

Pray... It is written of Your former deeds, O God, that
with a mighty hand You drove great nations from their lands
to establish a people holy to you. They defeated all enemies,
and no one could conquer Your chosen ones. Yet it was not
their strength that saved them but by Your might, through
Your favor, and by Your mere presence You rescued them.
As Your Father did then for His people, Lord Jesus, You command victory for me now. Through You I can defeat the evil
one, and by Your name I am able to put underfoot His forces
arrayed against me! Let me never trust in my own strength,
but in Your power to save me. By Your Spirit I can arise every morning to praise Your name. Indeed, let my boast be
of my God!

And yes, there are times when You have pruned and
corrected me—times when You let me suffer loss when
I desire victory and I have to wait when I want to charge
ahead. Sometimes I turn back in the face of the enemy, and
he takes the spoils of victory. Like a lamb I have been slain
because I wandered from Your side. I sold myself cheaply
to sin, bringing You no glory nor profit. I have become the
subject of mocking—the butt of jokes. My dishonor goes
before me, and the shame of my sin is not hidden. The voice
of the evil one taunts me, and all these the consequences
of my weakness. They come upon me for a season, to test
me. But as a child of Your covenant, let me not forget You
nor deal falsely. Let not my heart turn back, nor my hand
withdraw from the plow. Let not my steps depart from Your

way, rather let me learn obedience through the things I now suffer. Through all the tests, let me walk by faith and not by sight. When I deny Your name, or bow to idols, do You not search me out? You alone know the secrets of the heart and discern the thoughts of men. When I feel persecuted for my faith, let me remember what a blessing it is to suffer for Your name's sake. Awaken, O Lord! No longer stand aside but arise to my defense, so I no longer feel alone! Why does it seem at times You hide Your face and forget my trials? My soul is anxious, and my spirit is overwhelmed within me! Therefore, awaken to my help and renew me for Your names' sake.

Consider... *I am the Lord: the One forming light and creating darkness, causing well-being and creating calamity. I am the Lord who does all these.* This Psalm reveals both the kindness and severity of our God. He scatters and He retrieves and He tears down and builds up—scorching and then raising the scorched from the ash heap. We can endure, enjoy, or ignore His will, but we can never command it. We cannot possibly understand His plan at times, but if we press on the day will come when we look back and understand it all was for our good. Seek God diligently, maintain integrity, and brace yourself for the necessary wounds every disciple must incur. Walk into the darkness in faith, knowing that until the time He alone appoints you may "see only as in a mirror dimly." On the wings of your enduring faith, He will soon arouse Himself to command the victories that now seem so distant.

55(12-23)
Betrayal of the wolves

Pray... Lord, it is not those I would expect to oppose me who hear but do not understand. Their arrogance and ignorance I could bear. But You came to those who should have known You and they crucified You. It was those who walked and taught and held seats of honor in Your house who betrayed You—the lost sheep of the House of Israel who turned against You. May holy fear seize all who walk in Your house now, and the conviction of Your Spirit come upon us until repentance and wisdom turn us from their errors. Though we live in evil days, and walk among wicked generations, don't let those You have called unto You become lost in Your house once more. The lies of my true enemy do not change, and his false prophets do not fear You, for any light that may have been in them has become darkness. They stretch out their hands against those who desire peace as they trample underfoot Your covenant. The words of their mouths are smoother than butter, and temptation and deception have taken hold of their hearts. Their words are slicker than oil and they have become drawn swords penetrating the minds of the foolish, the babes, and the naive.

But as for me, let me call upon You, preaching and living the kingdom before the lost in Your house today as You did then. Salvation is in You alone, Lord Jesus. Lead me to pray without ceasing that You might hear my voice. You have redeemed my soul and given me peace in the midst of the conflicts that rage 'round about. The enemy bids me fight against flesh and blood, but You abide with me forever. You hear my prayers and take my battles upon Your broad shoulders. Cast your burdens upon the Lord, O my soul, and He shall sustain you! He makes the righteous steadfast, always abounding in His work because they know their efforts are not in vain. Your God will bring the false prophets down to the pit and deceitful men shall not arise to inherit eternal life. Only trust in the Lord for it is your lot to love the unlovely. Do not be overcome by evil, but rather overcome evil with the truth, goodness and righteousness.

Consider... *But My righteous one shall live by faith, and if he shrinks back My soul has no pleasure in him.* Just as the greatest joys of our faith can come from sweet fellowship, great damage can be done when falsehoods are proclaimed by deceivers in the body. While the overwhelming finality of grace cannot be denied, the biblical condemnation of those who insult that grace through the treachery of self-deceit and hypocrisy, the blasphemy and hard-heartedness of pride, or the lukewarmth of disobedience can neither be denied. There was only one group of people Jesus disdained—only one who would arouse His anger with their mere presence, and it was not the criminals, the prostitutes, or even the possessed. It was the religious hypocrites who should have been the first to recognize Him yet led the insurrection against Him. Beware false knowledge, for it is worse than ignorance and there is more hope for the ignorant than the one who says, "I see!" and yet does not. "And Jesus said to them, 'If you were blind, you would have no sin. But since you say, 'We see,' your sin remains.' The most dangerous ground of all to walk on, and the most dangerous people to embrace, those in whom the light has become darkness. Oh yes, how great is that darkness!

60

Times when He needs to break us

Pray... O God, prune and correct me, but I pray do not forget me. Though Your anger would be justified, remember Your covenant with me and restore me once again to grace. You make volcanoes spew forth, but then You heal the scars. You have shown me difficult times and given me paths to walk that make me stagger. Nevertheless, You have placed Your mark upon those who fear You because of trials endured, and hear Your voice and follow You, that Your truth might be manifested. They are Your holy ones, and You test and then heal. You crush and then deliver them. Deliver me with Your mighty right hand, O my God! Hear me, for You alone speak and act in holiness. You rejoiced as You measured out the earth and made the mountains and valleys. You created lands and nations, and they are all Yours. You have subjected them all to futility, but one day will restore them to the lordship of Your Son. One day all the faithful within them will come out, be separate, and shout in triumph because of what You have done!

Who will bring me into Your heavenly throne room? Who will lead me into Your kingdom on earth? Is it not Your Son's sacrifice and Your Spirit's calling, Lord? I was formerly dead in my trespasses and sins. We were estranged as I walked according to the ways of this world and lived by the spirit who works in the sons of disobedience. But then You sent Your Lamb to pay for my transgressions and bring me into His abiding presence. Now I know in whom I have believed and am convinced that You are able to guard what I have entrusted to You forever! You have shown me putting my trust in the kingdom of man and flesh is useless, and that through You alone I can have the victory over sin and death. You have destroyed the strongholds Satan once reserved for me! You have cleansed and forgiven me! You've called me out of the darkness and into Your marvelous light! Praise the Lord, O my soul, forever and ever for His mercies so new every morning!

Consider...*There shall be no resting place for the sole of your foot, but there the Lord will give you a trembling heart, failing of eyes, and despair of soul."* O brothers and sisters, we must not muzzle this Ox while He is threshing about in our lives! There are times when we need to feel the sting of God's pruning—to be shaken by His rod of correction driving us to our knees! To reawaken us to the fact that apart from Him we are truly helpless, He periodically appoints for us trials to endure that make us stagger. This is necessary, for those who know no defeat never learn to fear Him, and few lessons are ever well-learned in victory. We must let Him bring us into the source of our pain, and then lead us through our trial. When His goal for us is pruning, our best tutor is simply enduring faith. The trials and temptations of life that bring us to a trembling heart, failing of eyes, and despair of soul only serve to make us stronger if we allow that strength to be perfected in Him. God disciplines all He calls sons, so rejoice in the fact that you have been found worthy to suffer for His name's sake and be assured there are valuable lessons well-learned awaiting only on the other side of suffering's chasm.

62

Wait, and do not be greatly shaken

Pray… May my soul wait patiently, in truth and silence, to feel Your Spirit-wind. In You alone my renewal is at hand and my salvation is assured. You alone are the rock on which I stand and my safe harbor, for no other god holds eternal life in His hands. You grant me wisdom, so I need not be tossed about by the powers of darkness, the trickery of men, or the shifting winds of doctrine. The attacks of the evil one upon me are relentless, Lord! He conspires to bring me down from the high ground of Your kingdom. His people delight in lies—they bless outwardly with words while inwardly cursing. But they are to You as leaning walls and tottering fences.

O my soul, walk by faith and trust in Him. Wait patiently and peacefully for God alone, casting all your anxiety upon His Son, knowing He cares for you. Let your expectations fall upon His broad shoulders, for He alone is your anchor in the storm. He provides your defense and grants you everything for life and the pursuit of godliness. He keeps you from being led astray from the simplicity and purity of devotion and faith. In Jesus Christ alone your salvation and your glory abide! He is your rock of strength, so trust only in Him. Yes, my soul, trust in Him at all times and pour out your heart before Him, for He is your only refuge! Know that no one is to be looked down upon in His kingdom, and that desiring to be a person of high degree is vain and foolish. Do not trust in appearances, nor vainly hope in earthly gain. If riches increase, do not set your heart on them. If such earthly fare was weighed on God's scales, they would together be lighter than air. He has spoken once—twice you have heard this—true riches, truth, wisdom, might, honor, and glory belong to the Lord! Let mercy and justice reign, O God, as You render to each according to his faith and deeds.

Consider... *I did not withhold my heart from any pleasure...and behold, all was vanity and striving after wind.* In those moments born for patience and endurance, what is it that we wait for? Is it for riches to increase? Is it for power, gain, or fame? What is it that we look to for our hope? Have we sacrificed the joy we once knew in Christ because we would not wait in faith for the riches of the kingdom of heaven, and so went off vainly seeking the security of the riches of the kingdom of man? Were we shaken when we did not quickly see anticipated results, and so put our hope in worthless, worldly things? There is nothing more difficult sometimes than waiting upon the Lord, and this is the very reason that patience holds a seat of honor at the tables of love and the fruits of the Spirit and is key to the command of Jesus to be "perfect as His heavenly Father is perfect." We mustn't listen to Satan breathing lies in our ears, or envy others reaping earthly rewards. We cannot let our faith depend upon what we can see, smell, touch, and taste but rather ours is to wait in silence for God alone. Any substitute for waiting and trusting in faith amounts to striving after the winds of our own desires. Wait upon the Lord's divine plan, and you will not be greatly shaken!

63

My soul thirsts, and my spirit yearns for you

Pray... O God, You are my God. Early in the morning move my spirit to awaken to You, for You cause my soul to thirst for You and my spirit to long for You even in my dry and lonely seasons. I pray, grant me Your living water to sustain me during the droughts. Grant me endurance that I might press on toward perfection, to knock at heaven's gates that they might be opened to me, and to seek diligently Your kingdom that I might have rich fellowship with You! Through all let my heart remain steadfast, and my lips praise You, because Your presence is better than life itself. Let me bless You while I live, lifting up my hands to Your holy name. As though dining on a king's feast, let my soul be satisfied with Your presence. O God, let me count as joy all the trials of this life.

Bid me remember You as I lay down. Yes, lead me to meditate upon You in the night watches. In the shadow of Your wings I can rejoice, because I have been delivered! My feet can follow closely behind Yours as your presence upholds me and Your Spirit guides me. Nonetheless, Satan seeks me as the hunter would the prey. He dwells in the lower parts of the earth, seduces my flesh, and desires only to drag me down to destruction. Overcome his attacks by Your power, Lord Jesus. Show all looking on greater is He who is in me than he who is in this world. Grant him, and all those he has caused to deceive and rebel, the justice due them. But let me set my mind above where You are seated, find peace, and rejoice! As You shut the mouths of those who utter lies, let everyone who swears by Your holy name give praise!

Consider... *Ask and it shall be given to you. Seek and you shall find. Knock and it shall be opened to you.* Do we seek Him earnestly? Do our souls thirst for Him, and our spirits yearn for Him? "But seek first His kingdom and His righteousness, and all things shall be added to you." Until we are ready to realize we are not victims, but warriors ready to do whatever it takes to battle the powers of darkness with every gift of the Spirit and force of will—so totally identified with Jesus that He becomes the very air we breathe—the author and perfecter of our faith will still have some work to do. It is a dry and weary land that we live in on earth, but we can experience His mercies in the sanctuaries of abiding, peace in the safe harbor of His kingdom on earth, and His power in the fields of fruit-bearing if we are but willing to pay the disciple's price. Stopping short of the goal—"removing our hand from the plow and turning back"—will yield only the tasteless and unfulfilling lukewarm milk of babes, and we will wander off seeking our passions in worldly desires that will never satisfy. But if we will die daily at the cross, meet with the Spirit daily in a quiet place, and endure daily our appointed mission with joy, the evil one's plans will be impaled upon Jesus' flashing sword! Our soul's thirst will be satisfied with the tasty feast that is the disciple's reward.

70
The blessed affliction of the disciple

Pray... Come quickly, Lord Jesus, and deliver me from these trials and temptations. Make Your presence known now to me that I might be granted power in my inner man from on high. Fill me with Your peace that surpasses all human understanding that I might be able to stand against the thorns in my flesh. Confound and then defeat the evil one as he tempts and seeks my undoing. Yes, rebuke all his minions who seek to destroy, and turn away the thoughts that taunt, "Aha, aha, where now is Your God?" I am flawed, in need, and sin dwells in my flesh. But Your light which also dwells in me is greater, so do not delay making Your healing power known to me, O God!

Let all who seek You faithfully rejoice and be glad in You! Let those who love Your salvation continually proclaim, "The Lord Jesus Christ be magnified!" You are my help and my deliverer, so wait no longer. I know whom I have believed, and I am convinced that You are able to guard what I have entrusted to You until the very end. Oh yes, I know you guide my steps now, my redeemer lives, and in the end You, Lord Jesus—King of kings and Lord of lords—will take Your stand upon the earth to judge in righteousness and equity!

Consider... *We are fools for Christ's sake, but you are prudent in Christ. We are weak, but you are strong. You are distinguished, but we are without honor.* Disciples of Christ know that many times their lot in life is to be without honor for the sake of the honor of others. The Psalmists and the Apostles often speak of being afflicted, even as they encourage the rest of God's people to be strong, and this because God uses those more mature to suffer the fiery dart for those not yet able. Jesus Christ is the greatest example of this truth, for "surely our griefs He bore and our sorrows He carried. He was pierced through for our transgressions and crushed for our iniquities." It is all part of the sanctification process, that the practiced in Christ should carry the burden for those who are not. One is ready for leadership when "bearing another's burden, and so fulfilling the law of Christ," is what gives them their greatest joy even as it may cause them pain. Helping others to say, "Let Christ be magnified" as we shoulder the weight of their burden, is to be worthy of the mantle, "friend of Christ." This is the blessed affliction of the disciple, and the cross they gladly take up daily for the benefit of those less fortunate or less mature than themselves.

74

The enemy tears down our signposts

Pray... Lord, why does it seem at times You leave me adrift in this world and I no longer feel Your presence? I pray, remember my sonship through the covenant which You purchased with the blood of Your Son. Look down with mercy upon me, for the enemy seeks to pervert everything good within Your sanctuary. He roars within my soul as the powers of darkness set up their signposts as markers of my days! His false prophets spout their lies like loggers who lift axes in forests rich with trees, seeking to break down my defenses and set on fire truth and justice. They have defiled Your gathering places, seeking to destroy the witness of Your church. They suppress the Spirit in Your houses of worship, O God, and we no longer see encouraging signs. Our prophets are few, and no one among us knows how long the adversary will keep us captive. Will he be allowed to blaspheme Your name forever while it seems You stand at a distance with Your hand withdrawn?

Remove Your sword of indignation and justice from its sheath and shatter the darkness, for You are my King from of old who brought salvation out of death! Destroy the evil in Your might, break the chains that bind, and strike the heels of those who prophecy falsely! You bring forth both fountain and flood, and you dry up mighty rivers. The day is Yours, the night is also Yours, and You have prepared the light and created the sun that gives it. You have established the borders of the earth and made the seasons. Remember, Lord, how the enemy has mocked, and how the foolish who follow him have blasphemed Your name. Do not deliver the lives of Your innocent ones to this cunning opponent, nor forsake the hopes of the poor. Remember Your covenant, for Satan has created cruel traps for us in this flesh. Bring the oppressed back to You unashamed and lead the poor and needy to arise and praise Your name! Awaken, Lord Jesus, and plead Your own cause for Your name's sake! See how the proud mock You daily and forget not the taunts of Your enemies. The chaos of those who rise up against You is magnifying over the earth but blessed be our strong and merciful redeemer!

Consider... *Put on the full armor of God, that you may be able to stand firm against the devil's schemes.* It is very difficult sometimes to watch what's happening in the world and to the church and find reason to hope. It seems Satan has defiled everything, the bride's gown is tattered, and her eyes have grown dull. Our men "sleep and take their rest while the Son of Man is betrayed into the hands of sinners," and she has lost sight of her signposts. The absolute determination of our sworn enemy to damage everything within the house of God seems to be winning the day, leaving His sheep lost within her as they were when Jesus came. This is a prolonged fight with a tenacious opponent, whose own self-delusion will not allow him to admit defeat or cease in his battle. And though what we witness may make us want to give up we must not forget that God is in *absolute* control. His remnant, full of endurance and faith, always arises when the future looks bleakest. They press on, full of a greater Spirit and as emissaries of a greater cause, to light the way and keep our signposts before us.

77

Remembering God through fearful nights

Pray... Look and see, O Lord, I cry out to You knowing You hear me, and yet at times I still wonder. When sin and temptation surround and my soul is at war with flesh, I seek for You. Yet even as I search for strength and resolve I find no help. Still, I remember You and the pain of falling short of holiness makes me voice my complaint. My spirit becomes overwhelmed within me as I feel the sting of conviction. I become troubled and words to speak to You fail me. Sleepless, I search my heart and try to focus on more peaceful times, but my former songs of joy escape me. How I long for the peace of Your kingdom and of righteousness! I wonder, will You allow these thorns to prick me forever? Will I never know the healing You alone can offer? Have I lost favor in Your eyes, O God? Has the light of the promise of Your covenant dimmed? Have You forgotten to be gracious, and in judgement withheld Your desire to bless?

Yet, in my anguish I know I must cling to Your promises of mercy, keep my mind focused above, and remember the sum of Your works in my life. Surely now I must consider Your past wonders, meditate on all Your goodness to me and cling to what I know to be true. Shall I turn from the One who speaks the words of eternal life? Who is so great a God as You, the One who does wonders and reveals His strength in my weakness? Your sacrifice at Calvary has redeemed me and brought me m into Your kingdom. Your creation bears witness, O God—it looks to You and fears! Even the demons believe and shudder. Your voice thunders as it comes forth like a whirlwind and your light, like lightning, illumines the world as Your creation trembles! Your way is sometimes hidden from me, and the sum of Your thoughts will never be revealed to mere men. Surely, we see as in a mirror dimly and grasp vainly at mysteries. Nevertheless, in great mercy You emptied Yourself and came down from heaven to atone for our sin, write Your laws upon our hearts, and now we can have the very mind of Christ. You lead us forever as the sheep of Your pasture. Even in the darkness exalt and praise the name of your God, O my soul!

Consider... *If I do not do the works of My Father, do not believe Me. But if I do them, though you do not believe Me believe the works.* Times come when our spirits grow faint, we bow to the temptations of the flesh, and our souls know no comfort because we cannot seem to find God's presence anywhere. We cry out, "Will I will never know Your blessing again?" However, when our faith is shaken in the present, we can always draw upon the deep reservoirs of what Jesus has done for us in the past. Surely now we need to remember His wonders as a part of the complete tapestry the perfecter of our faith is weaving in our lives. Look back to Calvary—the greatest work ever done for you, and then look forward in faith renewed to fight again. See past your current trials to the works He is sure to do in your future. Trust in Him always for that future because of what you fully know to be true about the character and power your God has displayed thus far.

82 (& Matt 5)
Arise and judge for the meek

Pray...You alone reign in the congregations of the faithful, Lord! You sit in judgment over all lesser gods who are by nature no gods at all. But how long will they be allowed to deceive the hearts of the naive, promote lawlessness, and empower the wicked on the earth? In Your kingdom, Lord Jesus, the poor and fatherless have an advocate, and justice is served on behalf of the afflicted. Indeed, It is established and upheld in justice and righteousness! The lost and the downtrodden are delivered, freed from the hands of the wicked. The poor in spirit are blessed, for theirs is Your kingdom. Those who mourn are comforted and the gentle are granted an inheritance. Those who hunger and thirst for righteousness are also blessed and satisfied to the fullest. Under the government that rests upon Your shoulders, the merciful are granted mercy in return and the pure in heart clearly see and know You. The peacemakers and those who have been persecuted for the sake of righteousness, Your sons and daughters, are granted the keys and the gates of Hell shall not prevail against them.

Those who walk about in darkness do not know, nor do they understand. Forgive them, Lord, for they know not what they are doing. Show them how unstable the foundations of worldliness are, and that Your presence cannot abide in those who build upon them. You have said that we are gods, and all of us children of the Most-High. Nevertheless, apart from Your redemption we are but flesh, we shall die like mere men and be cast into the outer darkness forever. Whether we lived as paupers or princes, flesh will fail us. Arise, Lord Jesus, and come quickly to redeem those predestined for adoption as sons, and to judge the earth, for the world and all it contains is Yours!

Consider... *The Father has given all judgment to the Son, in order that all may honor the Son even as they honor Him.* We need to consider carefully the supreme authority and power of the One who came to judge as well as to save. The authority to redeem or cast into Hell did not cease when all became new, but passed from the Father to the One who earned the right through being tempted as a man and crucified for our sin to reconnect us to God. Jesus is now Lord over all our circumstances: political, societal, and personal. There is not some niche of existence that the Father withheld. There is nothing Jesus doesn't discern, understand, or preside over. We will all die like men, but the question remains how we will all live before then. And that is the reason the Lamb of God will rise up as the Lion and judge. He will take His rightful place, rendering judgment on all of those who said "Lord, Lord," yet practiced a decidedly different truth. He shall roar on the day He shakes the foundations of the earth, to divide His true followers whom He says will be "few," from false pretenders whom He says will be "many." Jesus said He did not come to abolish the law, but to fulfill it. And that law has always included the final judgment of *all* people. Do not be so foolish as to think the One who came to save us is not capable of damning us as well.

83

God's vengeance—our obedience

Pray... Do not keep silent, O God! Withhold Your judgments no longer and be still no more! Behold, Your enemy makes war against us and those who deny You have exalted themselves on the earth. Deceivers all, they have conspired against Your people and consulted together to seduce the naïve among them. They have said, "Come and let us cut them off that the name of Jesus may be heard no more." They have agreed with one mind, and now form a confederacy against You and Your elect. The principalities and powers of darkness, the unbelieving, the false prophets, and the wicked conspire amongst themselves to steal Your pastures from Your beloved sheep for their own selfish gain.

O my God, scatter them like whirling dust and like clouds before the wind! As the fire burns the woods, and as the flame sets the mountains ablaze, so pursue them in Your vengeance and subdue them with Your mighty power! Make their faces pale with fear, Lord Jesus, and fill them with conviction so perhaps some might turn, seek You, and live. But let those who stiffen their necks and harden their hearts be forever blinded and confused. Let them perish in the darkness reserved for them so that all may know that You, whose name alone is the Lord, are the Most-High over heaven and earth. As kingdom arises against kingdom, let them know You alone reign in righteousness and justice, and hold power over judgment, life, and death.

Consider... *If the world hates you, you know that it hated Me before it hated you. If you were of the world, the world would love its own. But because you are not of the world, therefore the world hates you.* Those under Satan's control share his contempt for us. It is their plan to conspire together with one mind to subvert and pervert our message. The only way to righteously deal with those who will not be saved is to not deal with them at all. Ours is to seek out, share the good news with, serve, and disciple those who may be saved, leaving vengeance up to Him. Jesus' command to us is that we serve them with our lives, share Him with our words, and wait for His Spirit to fill their hearts with conviction and hope. Only then will they be appalled by a newfound revelation of their sin and be overcome by His amazing grace. Obedience to the call of Jesus, not retaliation, is the way the disciple faces the world's hatred. To revile them in turn: matching law for law, sword thrust with sword thrust, and barb for barb, "do not even sinners do the same?"

84
Longing and yearning for His courts

Pray… How amazing is the tabernacle You have prepared in my heart through Your sacrifice, Lord Jesus. I have been bought with a price, therefore let me glorify You in word and deed. My soul longs, yes, even faints for Your abiding presence with me there. May my heart and my spirit cry out for You, my Living One! You give the sparrow a home and the swallow a nest where she may lay her young, but You care even more for me, numbering the very hairs of my head. How could I live in fear, for at Your altars O Lord, my King and my God, You have valued me far above all other creatures, both great and small?

Blessed are those who dwell in Your house to forever praise You! Blessed is the man whose strength is in You, and who has in his heart determined to follow You. He moves from strength to strength as he walks daily in Your Spirit. O Lord, God of Hosts, hear my prayer! Listen, O God of all creation and know You alone are my sword and shield in this battle! Look with favor upon the face of Your anointed, for truly a day in Your courts is better than a thousand anywhere else. Let me rather desire to be a doorkeeper in Your house than to dwell as a king in palaces of worldliness. You are my sun and my shield, and You alone give grace and bring glory. Indeed, You withhold nothing good from those who follow You with upright hearts You have made righteous. Lord Jesus, blessed is the man who trusts in You with all his heart, with all his soul, with all his mind, and with all his strength. Blessed is the man who abides in You and bears fruit that remains forever.

Consider... *The kingdom of heaven is like a treasure hidden in the field, which a man found and hid. From joy over it he goes and sells all that he has and buys that field.* If we could truly see what a day in the courts of God would be like—living in the very abode of blessing, beholding His face, and knowing fully His grace and glory for but a moment, we would trade that one moment for all the riches, power, and fame that the world could offer over a thousand lifetimes! We would truly count all we had here as rubbish. There is this sort of heaven on earth. Paul spoke of it when he said, "For *you* are our glory and joy...for now we really live if *you* stand firm in the Lord." If we want to catch a glimpse of heaven this side of the great divide, we simply need to pour the life of Christ that is now in us into others. We can find heaven working through us to the benefit of others in Jesus' love manifested right here on earth. Heaven on earth resides in this, because in this the Great Commandment is fulfilled. Abiding in His love is where His joy is found in us, and bearing fruit out of that love is where our joy is made complete. This is where we find Jesus' joy and enjoy the fellowship of other hearts on the highway to heaven, and that's as close to heaven as life on this earth ever gets.

86

He is good and ready to forgive

Pray... Hear my prayer, Lord Jesus. Listen, for my spirit is afflicted and my soul is needy within me. Anchor and strengthen my faith—remind me You have made me holy in Your sight and by Your stripes You have healed me. You are my God and the savior of all who follow and trust in You. As my soul cries out to You now, be merciful to me. Make glad the heart of Your servant as I lift it up to You. You are good and ready to forgive—so abundant in mercy to all who call upon You from a humble heart and a contrite spirit. So again I ask, hear my prayer and attend to my cries, for in troubled times no one else has the answers I seek. Among the gods of men there is none like You, nor are there any who can do works like Yours. Is there any god besides You, or is there any other rock? I know of none! All nations Your hands have fashioned shall come and worship before You. Every knee shall bow to glorify Your name, for You are the great I AM and You perform wonders!

Teach me Your ways that I might walk in Your truth. Unite my soul and spirit in the fear of Your holy name. O Lord my God. Let me praise You with all my heart and glorify Your name by bearing lasting fruit for Your kingdom on earth. Let me not hide my talents under rocks but invest them wisely for Your glory. Great is Your mercy toward me, for You have delivered my soul from the depths of Hell. The proud rise up against the righteous and the principalities of darkness seek our undoing. They shun Your presence in this world and in Your people. Yet You, O Lord, are a God full of compassion. You are gracious and patient—abundant in mercy and truth. I pray, turn to me and awaken my soul that Christ might shine on me anew! Grant me the strength to endure this good fight that I might be made perfect and complete, lacking in nothing. Show me a sign for good, Lord Jesus, so that those who do not believe may see it and be amazed! Then they will know You alone save, and Your Spirit alone helps and comforts Your people.

Consider... *"O Jerusalem, Jerusalem, who kills the prophets and stones those who are sent to her! How often I wanted to gather your children together...and you were unwilling."* Our God is good and ready to forgive, but so often we are unwilling. We listen to the lies of the evil one and begin to believe we have committed unforgivable sins. An image of Jesus forms in our minds as one unwilling or unable to grant us pardon. But that image we form is of us, and not Him. If we would but strive under grace to be godly, we could avoid much of the needless and persistent guilt that comes with hypocritical living. If we would do the good works He prepares that sanctify us, He would show us His promised signs for good, and "a multitude of sins would be covered." So much of our sorrow is self-inflicted, and so much of our doubt brought through our own disobedience. If we harden our hearts and close our ears to His persistent whispers calling us to action, we have no one to blame but ourselves. Though not without trial, there is grace aplenty for the disciple who keeps always an open ear, a repentant heart, and an obedient spirit.

88 *(with Isa. 53 & Phil. 2)*
In remembrance of the crucified Christ

Pray... Lord Jesus, author and perfecter of my salvation, You cried out in Your darkest hour, "My God, My God, why have You forsaken me? Why do You hide Your face from Me?" He heard Your prayers from heaven's throne, for Your soul had endured many troubles. You were drawing near to the pit of Hell, and about to be counted among those lost to the depths. Although You had existed in the form of God, You did not re-gard equality with Your Father a thing to be grasped, but emptied Yourself and came to us in the form of a bond-servant. Made in the likeness of men, You humbled Yourself through obedience to the point of death on a cross. You were despised and forsaken among men, counted among the dead. Like the slain in graves, whom God remembers no more, You were cut off from Your Father's hand. Then He put You in the lowest pit, pleased to crush You in the depths o0f the earth. His wrath rested upon You and He afflicted You with every sin of man, causing their transgressions to fall upon You. His burning anger passed over You and the terrors imposed nearly destroyed You. They washed over You like a flood and closed in on You from all sides. Your friends were taken far from You—they fled and said they did not know You. Those You came to save cried out, "Crucify Him!" You were oppressed and stricken, imprisoned and unable to find any way out. Your eye wasted away because of the burdens placed upon You as You suffered sin's wrath, but for our sake You endured, despising the shame.

Yes, even in the midst of unwarranted torment, You faithfully called upon Your Father. You spread out Your hands to Him, knowing You came to perform wonders for the dead, and that soon You would cause departed spirits to arise and praise His name. And because of Your sacrifice mercy was declared at the gates of hell, good news was preached to the formerly departed, and God's kingdom was secured on earth! Indeed, Your wonders were made known in the darkness and Your righteousness was manifested in the land of the forgotten. Because You presented Yourself a guilt offering You arose again to rejoice in Your legacy! Your rightful place was restored, Your Father established Your days forever, and His good pleasure now prospers in Your hand. As a result of the anguish of Your soul, Your Father looked on and was satisfied. By Your knowledge as His righteous one and faithful servant, You justified the many. You shed Your blood and bore our sins in Your body on the cross, that we might die to sin and live to righteousness! In the morning Your prayer came before Him, and through Your sacrifice we were delivered from the domain of darkness. We were transferred from darkness and certain death, and into Your glorious kingdom, that one day we might stand with the saints and cry, "Worthy, worthy is the Lamb!"

Consider... *He made Him who knew no sin to be sin on our behalf, that we might become the righteousness of God in Him—that [we] may know Him, and the power of His resurrection, and the fellowship of His sufferings.* Lest we forget the price by which we were purchased, let us meditate on these words and remember well this savior of ours. We tend to think because grace cost us nothing, it cost Him nothing. The anguish the Godhead must have experienced when the sin of the world mercilessly descended upon the spotless Lamb of God and the Father turned His back, is beyond human imagination. Picture the very foundation of an eternal relationship that had known nothing but oneness, love, and trust so severely shaken! How heart-breaking it was for Jesus to know the darkness, the helplessness, and the wretchedness of the human condition cast so undeservedly and forcefully upon Him, as it crushed Him so after living a sinless life. Oh, what travesty! Oh, what seeming injustice! But what genius, that in this injustice the most just strategy for the ultimate restoration of such undeserving, rebellious people as we was revealed! The crucifixion of all that was good brought about the resurrection of many who deserved it not. Have we truly connected with the cost of our salvation lately? He endured all this that "we may know Him, the power of His resurrection, and the fellowship of His sufferings." May we, one and all, take up our crosses daily in appreciation of this grace in which we stand. May it drive us to our knees, and then to our own sacrifice for our neighbor so that we never neglect so great a salvation!

89(38-52)
The lament of loneliness

Pray... Lord, I confess I feel distant from Your kingdom and its peace right now. Is it my sin that has put distance between us? I know You still care for me but I wonder where I stand because I do not sense Your presence, nor do I feel the joy or the life You came to give me in abundance. All my secure walls seem broken down and many hopes I had for this life remain unfulfilled. My peace has been too easily stolen, and I am treated by others with skepticism rather than understanding. It seems my tormentors have reason to rejoice, and the hand of my enemy has been loosed. I grow weary, my love grows cold, and my strength to fight the good fight wanes. I no longer feel Your glory, and my former shouts of victory have become but faint whispers. The strength and exuberance of youth is behind me and I feel weakened in Your Spirit under the stinging conviction of my sin.

How long, O Lord, will it feel as though You have hidden Your face? How long will it seem Your favor has been removed? Remember, I pray, how short my time is to bear fruit here for Your kingdom. Have You created and saved me for futility? Where is the abundant life You hold in Your hand? I cannot live and not see the grave, nor can I deliver my own flesh from the power of sin and death. It seems all has become vanity and striving after wind! My heart's desire is to feel the oneness with You I know is possible, but for now I can only grasp at fading memories for my hope. Lord Jesus, have mercy for Your servant struggles and remember how I despise the disgrace of my transgression! Consider also how

You came to defeat the power of sin for those predestined to glory, and to end the sting of death with which the enemies of the cross taunt me. In the midst of my suffering, let me stand on Your sure promises and boldly proclaim, "Blessed be the name of the Lord forevermore!" Amen.

Consider... *Truly, truly, I say to you, "When you were younger you used to gird yourself and walk wherever you wished. But when you grow old you will stretch out your hands, and someone else will gird you and bring you where you do not wish to go."* A prayer of desperation is sometimes all we can muster. When we bear in our souls the consequences of sin and are immersed in the shame of our fallen nature, it is many times only the "groanings of our spirits, too deep for words," that must suffice. Life following Jesus sometimes becomes this brought-to-ruin kind of existence, as it must be if we are to move from walking wherever we wish to finding that narrow path of faith He girds us for. Until we have been broken, the keenness of our faith has been blunted, we've wavered in battle, borne in our soul the reproach of our fallen nature, and alone gone out into the darkness and back with God, that path will continue to elude us. We will understand neither the depths of foolishness we are capable of when we gird ourselves, nor the power of God to gird us and take us where we do not wish to go for His ultimate glory. Yet it is precisely the path we must be willing to endure for the sake of the Gospel and the tribulations we must conquer to enter the kingdom.

A Poem: Though He Slay Me

Though God slay me—though He lay my faith in dust
Challenge all in me that once brought me to Him trust
When all that I thought given He now hastens to take
When all I thought blessing He now says, "Son, forsake"
When the narrow path, once visible and straight
Leads only to barred and forbidden gate
When hope turns to ashes,
and my glory before my brethren to spite
And all former mountaintops fade far from my sight
Yes, when and not though He take me from His rest
And send me naked and bleeding into one more grievous test
Will I then arise on the wings of pride?
With my flesh will I then side?
Casting all past lessons behind me
For a bowl of Pottage will I sell all I knew so cheaply?
Do I bargain my birthright for solace today
Forgetting the greater sufferings of the
One who girded and brought me this way?
Nay, for I'd rather be a doorkeeper in His house and eat
crumbs falling from His table
Than to dine with the worldly-
well and drink with the worldly-able
O my soul, if this is the lot that falls unto you
The die that is cast and the cross you must carry
Then grasp it with both hands, singing songs while you plow
Never minding the sores you find there,
nor the sweat that drips from your brow
Though it seems not a particularly fertile field
'Tis yours only to sow and water, but
Christ's alone His fruits to yield
Does the thing molded say to its Potter,
"For what purpose hast Thou made me?"

Does the freedman, once the slave, say to his liberator,
"Why hast Thou saved me?"
Nay, for though He slay me yet must I praise Him
For whatever light now dispatches my total darkness, be it
faintest candle or highest beam
Light is better than the darkness, be it blinding or be it dim
Yea, though He slay me 'tis not mine to complain
For I must trade all this world has to offer for but crumbs
received in His name

102(1-18)
He is gracious to the desperate

Pray... Hear my prayer, Lord, and let my cry come before You. Please don't seem distant in my day of trouble, but rather hear and draw near. Answer me quickly for my days are consumed in a fog and my faith waivers in the temptations of unholy desires. My heart is stricken, and my peace shaken. My zeal for life wanes, I feel nothing, and hear only the sounds of my groanings. I am like a lonely bird in the wilderness and a wanderer in barren deserts. I lie awake, alone at night, stranded and teetering on the brink. The enemy relentlessly mocks me, reminding me of my destruction which he has sworn an oath to. I have tasted of the bitter ashes of sin and drunk from the cup of failure. I feel worthy only of Your indignation and judgment, fully deserving of my anxiety and despair. My days are like a shadow that never recedes into the light. Hope fades within the dark and hidden recesses of my soul.

Nevertheless, Lord Jesus, I know Your tender mercies endure forever. You have made known to every generation the grace and salvation that is in Your name alone. Indeed, You always stand ready to show mercy to Your people, so I pray let the time of Your favor come quickly. As You have mercy on me, I will be able to endure this fight, for I know You regard the prayers of those who are hurting and will honor their requests. Your presence shall return and restore me, and one day You shall appear to me in Your glory. Teach me to fear Your holy name and stand in awe of the One In whom I can trust! You have established Your covenant for generations to come, that a people yet to be created may arise to praise You! Bring me out of this slumber and awaken me from this death that Christ might shine upon me and I might proclaim the power of Your grace! A battered reed let me not be broken off, and a smoldering wick let me not be put out until You lead justice and mercy to victory!

Consider...*For since He Himself was tempted in that which He has suffered, He is able to come to the aid of those who are tempted.* This graphic description of human doubt and fear reveals that even those after God's own heart can suffer desperate times. Jesus knew desperation on our behalf, as indeed He was made to endure all human sufferings for our sake. Thankfully, He still stands tall as the One tempted on our behalf who sinlessly endured every attack and gives us constant hope and strength through the battles, along with mercy when we succumb at times. But we must remember desperate lives is not what He created us for, but rather for love and peace and joy! He says to those who wallow in the shadows, "Awake, sleeper, and arise from the dead that I might shine upon you!" We will always be able to find healing if we get out of ourselves within the fellowship and work of His saints if we seek, knock, and ask. The One who was tempted in all things is now able to come mercifully to our aid, lift us up, and make us shine anew in His Spirit!

109 *(1-20)*
A prayer for protection

Pray... Do not keep silent, O God of my worship, for the jaws of wickedness and deceit open wide to strike! With a lying tongue the evil one whispers in my ear. He taunts my soul with words of darkness as he assaults the faithful and advances his twisted cause. Because he knows I love You, he accuses me day and night before Your throne, but I know You live to make intercession for me. Therefore, let me give myself to prayer, seeking Your kingdom, abiding in Your love, and calling upon Your nearness. Satan has rewarded me evil for good and returned only hatred for my faith in You. The wicked man stands to his right hand and the accuser to his left. He has been judged and found guilty, and sinful are the chants of his people. Let his days be few, Lord, as You rip his kingdom mercilessly from his grasp! Let his servants, who go out deceiving and being deceived, return to him empty-handed. May they wander about, useless and begging in desolate places.

You are his creditor, Lord, so seize all that he has! Call Your saints to plunder his labor and let no one succumb to his deceptions. Those who follow him shall know no favor beyond this life, for he shows no mercy and cannot save. He persecutes the poor and needy and seeks to slay the broken in heart. But his legacy shall be cut off, and when You come in glory the memory of his name shall be erased forevermore. Let the evil he has caused remain fresh in Your memory and do not forget the evil he has loosed on earth. Keep his offenses continually in mind and cut off the legacy of his wickedness from the earth. Bring the cursing and deception he loves so back to rest upon him. He does not delight in blessing so let blessing be taken from him. Wickedness is the cloak which forever covers him, the oil that forever anoints him, and the chain with which he will be forever bound. May this be the reward for this one who stands against me, tempts me with sin, and utters his lies to my weary soul.

Consider... *Then the Lord knows how to rescue the godly from temptation, and to keep the unrighteous under punishment for the Day of Judgment.* Too often we adopt a false image of Satan as a passive, part time hunter and that's precisely what he desires. This is no cartoon character with pitchfork in hand, clad in red pajamas bidding us to a party down under. This is a tenacious, vile, and imminently dangerous beast: beautiful in appearance and wickedly cunning. He will mercilessly attack anywhere, at any time, and by any method, be it cruelty or kindness, abundance or want, victory or defeat. The common denominator will be deception, for he is the Father of Lies. He's on the job full-time, ever vigilant to find that one opening he craves. We are no match for him apart from total reliance on the power of the greater One alive in us. Don't fall to naivety but ask God to open your eyes to the desperate war being waged for your soul. Understand that He knows how to rescue you from Satan's many schemes, and exactly what to do with those who would join him in un-tracking your faith. Always be as vigilant as he is in fighting the good fight for your soul!

109 (21-31)
Being glad when afflicted

Pray... Lord Jesus, my savior and my God, show mercy to me for Your name's sake, for while I am a saint at times I wander from Your paths. In all Your ways, You are full of compassion and Your mercy is full of goodness. Therefore, deliver me for I am broken and within me my spirit needs Your healing touch. Sometimes my soul is stricken with temptations, doubts, and fears. The shadows of darkness lengthen over me, and my faith is shaken. I am not at home in religion's temples—they shake their heads at me. Nevertheless, let me honor You alone with fasting and prayer, that my flesh might not prevail over me. Help me, O Lord my God, and renew me according to Your mercy, that all may know it is Your hand that raises me up. You alone can forgive me when I stumble and cause all things to work together for good for me because I love You and am called according to Your purpose. Indeed, You have done all for me and given me everything pertaining to life and godliness.

Though the world may curse me, and my flesh and my fears betray me, I pray You would remember Your covenant with me. When evil rises up against me let it not gain the victory, but in all things give me cause to rejoice! Let the one who accuses me know only failure and defeat. Turn him away and reveal his disgrace, that I might lift up my voice in praise once again! Let me praise You in Your Ecclesia, for You stand at the right hand of the afflicted and save them from oppression.

Consider... *Consider it all joy, my brethren, when you encounter various trials, knowing that the testing of your faith produces endurance. And let endurance have its perfect result, that you may be perfect and complete—lacking in nothing.* There is no greater promise in all of Scripture than this. What more all-inclusive promise could God make, than to present us perfect and complete before Him? What could be better than to be found "lacking in nothing?" These rewards are not found in preaching, teaching, healing, or in any of the manifestations of spiritual gifts, as worthy as such pursuits may be. Drawing near to perfection will never come through enjoying the blessings of our faith if we fold under the weight of enduring the trials of our faith. Daily putting one foot-of-faith in front of the other as we endure our tests, all the while abiding in Him and bearing His fruit, is where perfection for the saint is found. Enjoying blessings requires little faith. Bearing trials joyfully, not the least of which is the war raging on between flesh and spirit within, requires great faith. It is only when we press on with wounded hearts, weakened knees, and shaken confidence that we understand what it means to walk by faith and approach the perfection He seeks for us, because it is only then *His* power is perfected in us. We need to count everything given us from the hand of God as joy—all of it—both mountaintop and valley. Those who do will be faithful witnesses existing to be credible testimonies of how He keeps his covenant.

116

Return to your rest, O my soul

Pray... I love You, Lord Jesus, because You first loved me. You hear the longings of my heart and receive my prayers. Because You care for me, I know I can call upon You as long as I live. When the confusion of deception surrounds me, the pangs of temptation entice me, and I find myself in the midst of trouble, doubt, and sorrow, I can call out Your name and be delivered from discouragement's grasp. Gracious and righteous are You, Lord Jesus, for as far as the east is from the west You have removed my sin from me. Oh yes, my God is merciful, preserving the simple and rescuing the lowly. And so, return to your rest, O my soul, and fear not for the Lord Jesus, rich in mercy, has dealt oh, so graciously with you! He has delivered you from the law of sin and death, and given you life in the Spirit, for precious in His sight is the sanctification of His saints. He has removed the tears from your eyes and the stumbling blocks from before your feet. I believe, Lord, and yet still at times am afflicted. In my alarm I curse with my mouth and stumble on my feet, but You are faithful to forgive me and cleanse me from all unrighteousness. O God, let me be like You, never returning evil for evil, that I might walk before You forever in the land of the living.

What then shall I give in return for all You have given to me? Let me take up the cup of salvation, walk in Your kingdom, and dwell in the power of Your Spirit as I call upon Your name. May I live as a disciple who observes all You command in the presence of Your people, striving to maintain a clear conscience before both You and my brothers! Lord, truly make me Your servant who lives as one who appreciates the loosing of the bonds that held me captive as a slave to sin. Call me out to offer to You a sacrifice of thanksgiving, praising and worshipping Your holy name! May I be a son of integrity in the presence of all Your people gathered in Your courts—in the midst of the church of the living God, boldly declaring "Praise the Lord, O my soul!"

Consider... *Come to Me all who are weary and heavy-laden, and I will give you rest. Take My yoke upon you and learn from Me, for I am gentle and humble in heart, and you shall find rest for your souls.* It is the good fight, is it not, to hold fast to that good confession and display integrity in the presence of His people regardless of what befalls us? And what a fight it can become! The closer we get to God as we start sharing that good confession, the harder Satan presses the guiles of Hell upon us. But God always counts precious those who call upon Him in the heat of the good fight. He stands ready to save, ready to preserve, ready to restore us to the peace of the kingdom, and ready to return our souls to His rest when we have suffered injury. As we return from the wars greatly afflicted, having fulfilled our commitments to Him in the presence of all, He proudly receives us with "Well done, good and faithful servant. Walk before Me always in the land of the living."

A Poem: Return to Your Rest

Return to your rest, O my soul,
in the midst of your afflictions
Return to your rest, from your heart's
woundedness within
Return to your rest even as your
faith is sorely shaken
When you are weakened, and your
hopes dashed on the rocks of your sin
When you say, "All men are liars,"
you serve only to fan judgment's fires
When you join the evil in cursing,
it is only your flesh you are nursing
Rather, my soul, cry out to God,
"Lord, renew my strength
And again remind me what is the depth,
breadth, and length
Of the love that came in
spite of the evil within me
That, while I was yet sinner,
conspired so mercifully my soul to free!"
And when Satan arises, curses only to employ
May I see through His scheming to hope, love, and joy
Finding contentment, whatever my lot
Not looking to who I perceive I am, or am not
To singing Your praises in the tents of the forgotten
The least of these so oppressed and down-trodden
For Your sake, O Lord, and for Your name alone
Deal kindly with me, and do for
my transgressions ceaselessly atone
Through that yoke that upon me is easy and light
Granting such peace in the midst of the fight
That I might endure every trial, acquit well every test
That You may say to my soul, "Now return to your rest"

119(17-32)
His words our counselors

Pray... Make Your mercy and blessings known to me, Lord, that I might live to keep Your Word, for hope deferred makes the heart sick. Open spiritual eyes in me that behold wondrous things from Your truths! You have made me a stranger on this earth, for now I desire a better, heavenly country. Grant a revelation of Your truths in my spirit and give me a never-ending desire to have and know the mind of Christ. You rebuke the proud and correct all who stray from Your commandments. Shelter me, O God, from the contempt of man and the condemnation it can bring as I strive to walk in Your ways. Although those in seats of power may mock and speak out against me, let me meditate on Your Word, day and night, and find peace. Ignoring their taunts, let me walk in the light as You are in the light, always striving to make Your story my delight and Your words my counselors. My soul would dwell in the depths if You did not uphold and sustain me according to Your promises. May I never deny You before men, but rather reveal my commitment to You in all my words and deeds.

Answer me when I call, Lord, and teach me to walk in Your commands. Help me to understand the way of Your Word, that I might have an answer for everyone who asks. And when my soul is weighed down with sin's burdens, grant me repentance and mercy, strengthening me according to Your Word. Remove from me the lying way and graciously grant me wise understanding of Your truths. Lead me to choose the way of truth by faithfully walking in Your righteousness, transformed by the renewing of my mind. Bid me cling to Your testimonies, O God, lest after I have shared Your truth with others I would be disqualified. I desire to run in such a way that I may win the prize, for then I would travel on the highway of holiness, and You would enlarge my heart!

Consider... *Take to your heart all the words with which I am warning you today—even all the words of this law—for it is not an idle word for you. Indeed, it is your life.* Living by every word that proceeds from the mouth of God is the only way to find life. There can be no substitute, nor end run—no alternate route to sanctification. It is through meditating upon *and* practicing His Word we mature. It is Jesus Himself we abide in when the Word becomes manifest in our lives, for He is "the Word made flesh." But His Word will not share the throne-of-our-hearts with pride, because running with His Word enlarges our heart, while pride and arrogance hardens it. When we choose to run to the way of His words—meditating on, and making them our constant counselors—He enlarges our hearts that we may love the unlovely, endure the ungodly, and walk as He walked in this world. Then the world sees the Word made flesh in us. Then the world sees Jesus, He is lifted up, and all men are drawn unto Him.

119 *(33-48)*
The answer for those who question

Pray... Teach me the way of righteousness, O Lord, that I might walk in it. Give me the mind of Christ that You might instruct me, and understanding and wisdom that I might be called Your disciple. May I lay aside every encumbrance, running with endurance and a whole heart the race You have set before me. Bring me to walk on the narrow path that leads to life, and to keep Your commands because I delight in them. Give me a heart that desires Your truths and revive me in Your Holy Spirit. Keep me from coveting what others have and turn my eyes away from looking at worthless things. May Your Word abide firmly in my heart, bringing me to revere Your holy name above all else. Turn away guilt and shame and help me to understand it is only for my good that You discipline me.

I long for Your Word revealed in my heart. Yes, my soul pants for Your revelation! Revive me in Your righteousness, O Lord, and let Your tender mercies comfort me. When I am weary grant me Your yoke that is light and Your burden that is easy. Bring to mind the assurance of Your kingdom promised to me in Your Word. May I always have an answer for all who question because I trust fully in Your promises. When asked to give a reason for the hope that is within me, let Your Spirit speak through me with boldness! O Lord, I pray do not allow Your words of truth to escape my heart and my testimony, for they are my hope in this world. Bring me to abide in You continually, take up my cross daily, deny my selfish desires enduringly, and follow You fully as long as

I shall live. Then Your Word shall set me free indeed and I shall walk in liberty. May I never deny You, but rather speak Your truths before kings and common men alike as one unashamed of Your Gospel. May I always love Your Word and lift up my hands to Your holy laws. Lead me, O Lord, to meditate upon and keep Your teachings.

Consider... *But sanctify the Lord God in your hearts, and always be ready to give a defense to everyone who asks you the reason for the hope that is in you.* It is the supreme test of our faith in God's holy Word, that we trust it enough not only to see us through our own trials [as we abide in Jesus], but also for the salvation and sanctification of others [as we bear fruit]. Do we trust the Word in our own lives, but then look to worldly solutions or fall silent altogether when others need our counsel? Is it merely our private truth, or do we have faith enough in it that it becomes sufficient for all? Do we love our neighbors as ourselves, enough to share with them the truths of God we have come to believe? We gain valuable knowledge when we seek His truth, but we learn to love His Word only when it bears fruit through us because it has become the answer to our life's story for all who would question.

119(81-96)
The consummation of all perfection

Pray... Lord Jesus, my soul faints as I long for You to make known Your plan to me. Let me wait in faith for the promise of Your kingdom and hope in Your presence to comfort me. May my eyes fail from searching Your Word as I seek Your peace and comfort. When I become like a flower withering in the summer's heat, I know I must not forget Your promises. How many are the days left to me to bear fruit on this earth? When will You bring judgment upon the evil that sets traps for You're people? I long to act according to Your plan, and to fulfill my purpose. All Your teachings are faithful, and I desire to keep them, yet Satan hinders and patience fails. So, help me my Lord, for greater are You than this evil one who seeks to steal, kill, and destroy. I know if I do not forsake Your commands, You will revive me according to Your mercy and promise. By Your grace, and the power I receive through Your Spirit, I have all I need to keep the way You have established for me.

Forever, Lord, your Word is settled in heaven. Forever Your faithfulness endures on earth. You established the world and so it remains. Everything in Your creation exists and lives to serve You, day by day, according to Your plan. Unless Your Word had been my delight, I would have succumbed to the blows of evil's afflictions. But You have not allowed me to forget Your truths, and through them You have given me new hope. You have purchased me back from the grave and I am Yours. Therefore, let me live to seek Your kingdom and display my gratitude by loving others as

You have loved me. The wicked one waits to undo me—he prowls about like a Lion ready to pounce, so let me always treasure Your Word in my heart and have Your praises upon my lips. This is my heart's prayer, for I have seen the consummation of all perfection in Your kingdom, so very good!

Consider... *Man shall not live by bread alone, but by every word that proceeds from the mouth of God.* While human history is beset with turmoil, the Living Word rules in heaven. Isaiah 9 tells us we have a very different government filled with peace that is being ruled daily "in justice and righteousness. This is why Jesus taught us to pray, "Thy will be done on earth as it is in heaven." The Living Word, who came to earth in the form of His Son, will one day settle all things on earth as they are now in heaven. Until then, we can know the peace of this heaven on earth where, if we truly believe Jesus is ruling, nothing is in chaos, out of control or worthy of our worry. Let us hold fast to one Lord, one faith, one baptism, and one God and Father of all who is over all and through all and in all. Most critically, we must not allow ourselves to step out of His kingdom and back into mans', where we open ourselves to the attacks of the prince of darkness once more. When the proud one digs pits for us with his lies, and we cry out to God, "When will You comfort us?" we must renew our perspective as to which kingdom we are of. The consummation of all perfection on earth now can be what it will be in eternity then and that is heaven brought to earth. But we must, as He said, "seek it first."

119 *(120-131)*
Light to the simple

Pray...Lead me to work out my salvation in fear and trembling, Lord—to speak and act upon this earth as one who reveres Your holy laws, for not one stroke of the letter of the law shall ever fail. May holy fear and an appreciation of grace lead me to do justice, love righteousness, and lay down my life for others. Deliver me from sin, be my guarantee of goodness in this world, and let not the boastful pride of life defeat me. May my eyes fail from seeking wisdom and discernment in Your words of righteousness. Deal with me in mercy and judge not according to my sin, nor chasten me according to what I deserve. Teach me Your truths and make me Your servant. Give me good understanding that I may know and walk in Your every desire for me.

I pray Lord, rebuke those who do not fear You and willfully break Your laws. Chasten and admonish those who say, "Lord, Lord" and yet practice lives of lawlessness. But let me love Your kingdom more than gold, being all the more diligent to make my calling and election sure. I consider Your truths to be right in every way, and by Your Spirit I learn to despise every false way. Your testimonies are wonderful and therefore I can keep them with a clear conscience. The introduction of Your words gives light and understanding to the simple, for You have chosen the foolish things of the world to shame the wise and the weak things of the world to shame those that are strong. How I long for Your truth and the power to walk on Your paths, for it keeps the power of sin from having dominion over me.

Consider... *But I am afraid, lest as the serpent deceived Eve by his craftiness, your minds should be led astray from the simplicity and purity of devotion to Christ.* It is the simplicity and purity of our devotion to Christ that keeps us walking in one simple command of our Lord, "Seek first His kingdom and His righteousness." Adam listened for just a moment to the deceiver of humankind as he turned from the one simple command God gave him and he fell. When we refuse to heed His simple, written disciplines: abiding in Jesus and His Word, lending our gifts to the edification of the fellowship, and being and bearing lasting fruit in the world, He cannot trust us with the meatier fare of hearing His voice and entrance to His kingdom on earth. It is abiding in and spreading His pure, righteous, faithful, light-giving, and yet simple message through word and deed that keeps our eyes off of the tree of the knowledge of good and evil, and firmly focused on the Tree of Life. The crafty one desires to confound us by making God's truths seem so complicated, and a simple mission so difficult. Unfold His Word today, deem it right concerning every single thing, ask for discernment to hate every false way, and call upon His power to seek first His kingdom. Yes, "Repent, for the kingdom of heaven is at hand!" In unfolding and acting upon His Word, both written and revealed, there is light and understanding—simple.

119*(145-165)*
Revived by His Word

Pray... As I offer up the desires of my heart hear me, Lord Jesus! Empower me to be obedient to Your Word. I cry out to You, the only One who saves, that I might be renewed to be one You call "friend." Let me rise before the dawn to offer prayers and petitions for help, hoping in Your presence for strength. May I remain ever alert to the darkness, meditating on Your Word. In Your tender mercies hear my cries, O Lord, and by Your grace revive me. The powers of darkness draw near, ordaining the footsteps for the wicked who remain distant from Your truths. But Your Spirit is nearer, in my heart and on my mind, and all of Your counsel is good and true. From antiquity You have made it known, O God, that Your Word will always stand firm, therefore let me never forget. Consider my trials and deliver me, Lord Jesus. Plead my cause, for I know You live to intercede for me before Your Father. Redeem me and revive my spirit through Your Spirit.

Salvation is far from the wicked, for they do not seek Your truth and it is spiritually discerned from them. But great are Your tender mercies towards all who call upon You from a heart made pure and a conscience made blameless. O Lord, revive me in Your merciful way, for many are the temptations Satan brings to bear. Let me never turn to the right nor to the left from Your narrow path. I see the treacherous one persuading the naïve and I weep because he keeps them in darkness, unable to understand Your truths. Consider how I love the lost sheep of Your house and revive me in Your mercy and grace. The entirety of Your Word is truth, and every one of Your righteous judgments is everlasting. Though the prince of darkness may persecute me with evil intent, continue to fill my heart with awe for You. Bid me rejoice in Your kingdom as one who has found great treasure and will gladly sell all he has to purchase it. May my spirit love Your truths and resist Satan's lies. Daily call me to praise You because of Your righteous and just way. Those who live in Your kingdom know great peace. They do not find Your commands to be burdensome, but live by them, and nothing causes them to stray from Your abiding presence.

Consider... *The Lord God has given me the tongue of disciples, that I may know how to sustain the weary one with a word.*
All the disciple of Christ needs to revive the lost [saved or not] is a Word from the Spirit and His living love. If we rejoice over the pearl of great price that is His kingdom, it becomes ever the source of our strength and peace. If we meditate upon and abide in His words to us, then the One who is the Word will be faithful to abide in us. "If His Word abides in us, and we in Him, we shall ask whatever we wish and it shall be done for us," and this because our request will be according to His will. If we shod our feet with the gospel of peace, awaken before dawn to cry for help, and then wait patiently for His promises to manifest themselves in our lives, we will be able to stand and resist in the evil day. Love the Living Word, Jesus Christ, the Word made flesh, and be renewed! Find your peace and wisdom in His kingdom, and He will not allow the enemy's deceptions to win the day!

119 *(166-176)*
Never forgetting His commandments

Pray... Lord, as I strive to walk with You in the power of Your Spirit, my hope lays in the promise of Your kingdom come. May my soul pay heed to Your instruction and my heart love Your ways above all else. Let it be said of me that I kept Your Word and walked in it, and that my ways were righteous before You. Let my cry come before You, O God— grant me understanding and wisdom! Oh, hear my prayer and consider my requests according to Your sure promises!

I pray, do not allow me to be tempted beyond what I am able to bear in this world. Lead me not into temptation but deliver me from evil for the glory of Your name! Let my lips proclaim Your praises, for You have taught me and upheld me in Your truths. May I never remove my hand from the plow and withdraw, rather let my tongue forever proclaim Your Word. Lord Jesus, all Your commands are righteousness and in them I find the light that sets me free. May Your presence be my everlasting and sufficient help, leading me to choose to walk in Your kingdom on earth. I long for Your abundant life, Lord, therefore let Your words and ways be my delight. Command my soul to live to praise You, and let Your Spirit be my guiding light. When I go astray like a lost sheep, and like a prodigal son, seek me out, lead me to repentance, forgive my every sin, and correct and train me anew in righteousness. Let me never forget Your commandments, O God. Rather, let me prove my love for You by keeping them with great joy!

Consider... *So watch yourselves, lest you forget the covenant of the Lord your God which He made with you.* It is fitting that the final words ["Let me never forget Your commandments."] of the longest chapter of the Bible should summarize its message so well, for the longest chapter in God's Word is wholly *about* His Word. We cannot possibly be keepers of the Great Commandment without a divinely inspired love for, and a passionate and practical pursuit of, His Word, both revealed and spoken to us. John said, "This is the love of God: that we keep His commandments, and His commandments are not burdensome." Jesus' true friends mature to a place where they love His commands and keep them with a cheerful heart. And how could they not? It's not their heart at all, but His beating gladly within them. How could the Spirit, whom Christ sent and speaks to us through not love His own commands? Do not be deceived: you love His commands and they are never a burden because you walk in the Spirit, or you find them a burden because you walk in the flesh, for the flesh hates God's commands. Though discipline is where the race must begin (Heb. 12:11), the goal is to grow more fully into a relationship where Jesus is the One doing His own will through us. When His words abide in us by the Spirit whom He has given us, keeping them ceases to be a discipline and increasingly we yield to the peaceful fruit of righteousness which was the goal of the discipline from the beginning. This is when the Word—Jesus Himself—becomes our life and joy!

123 (& Rom. 7)
A sinner's prayer for mercy

Pray... Unto You I lift up my eyes—unto my God who dwells in heaven yet lives within me. To You I submit and grant rule over my soul. As the eyes of servants look to the hand of their master, and the eyes of sheep to their shepherd, so let me seek You out until the time temporary trials pass, healing comes, and Your revelation dawns anew in my spirit! Have mercy on me, O Lord! Have mercy on me, for I do not know what I do at times. What I want to do I don't do, and that which I hate is the very thing I do. Therefore, I know it is not I who do it but sin that dwells within my flesh. Let this be a constant reminder to me that nothing good dwells there, for I desire to do right yet at times I become filled with evil desires that overcome me. I become jealous of those who seem to live carefree, successful lives even as I wait for my dreams. You fill me with conviction over my sin, yet at times I succumb to the lusts of my flesh and my eyes. Many times, with tears and petitions, I seek deliverance and yet it eludes me. I hear only, "My grace is sufficient for you, for in your weakness My power is perfected."

Oh, wretched one that I can be, foremost of sinners! Who but You can deliver me from this body of death? And You do, Lord, for even in my lowly estate You help me rise up to give thanks for grace. As I confess my sins, even again and again, You are faithful to forgive me and to remove my stains. Have mercy on me, O Lord! Have mercy on me, for this enemy within my flesh never sleeps nor slumbers. And yet, my heart's desire is only to hear, "Well done, good and faithful servant."

Consider... *But as for me, my feet came close to stumbling, for I was envious of the arrogant as I saw the prosperity of the wicked. Do not fret because of evildoers and be not envious toward wrongdoers. Commit your way to the Lord—trust also in Him and He will do it.* Even the greatest of Scripture's saints struggled mightily with the flesh. This battle that rages between flesh and spirit seems at times to leave us helpless bystanders to the struggle between the forces of heaven and hell. We feel so powerless against those "thorns in our flesh," as we follow our desires into places we know we should not go. We know we're putting ourselves in harm's way and will be sorry for it later, but we proceed anyway. We know what we are about to do is wrong, and it would defeat our witness for Christ and cause collateral damage to the ones we love, but we have made that choice and it doesn't seem to matter. Sin dwells within us, no matter how disciplined or spiritual we may become. But Jesus gave us two ways to fight sin: inwardly we must remain repentant and not let ourselves rationalize or justify sin, for this leads us down the slippery slope of superficiality into lawlessness. Outwardly, we must not let the knowledge of our weakness dissuade us from those good deeds that, like repentance, also "cover a multitude of sins." We must endure, running the race well to the finish line, for it is this that perfects and brings us into His kingdom.

130
He does not mark our iniquities

Pray... At times I must cry out to You from the depths of temptation and sin, Lord, hoping You will hear my voice and answer my prayers. If You were to keep score of my iniquities—if You were to mark them in Your book, how could I ever stand before You or even come into Your presence? But You deserve all glory, for You are the God of mercy and forgiveness, and I have been redeemed through Your blood according to the riches of Your grace! I can stand in awe and worship, steadfastly waiting upon You in trust and faith, for I know it is no longer I who sins but sin working through my flesh. May my soul wait patiently and forever hope in Your promises, Lord Jesus, knowing You died to save me from my sin and through repentance the door to cleansing is always open. May I watch for You more than those who eagerly await the morning, and may I persevere beyond those who patiently watch for the coming of night.

O church of the living God, hope forevermore in the Lord! Refuse to be anxious, pursue the peace of His kingdom, in everything through prayer and supplication with thanksgiving let your requests be made known to Him, and then patiently wait. With You, O Lord, there is mercy, for You alone hold redemption in Your hand. You redeem all who wait upon You from their iniquities, and You are the hope of all who fear You and endure trials and temptations. Your peace, surpassing all human understanding, guards their hearts and minds in Your Son Jesus. Praise the Lord, O my soul, for His everlasting love and kindness towards you!

Consider... *As far as the east is from the west, so far has He removed our transgressions from us.* How blessed we are that our God does not keep a running tab on our debt. How solid is our hope that when we go to Him with repentant hearts, He forgives us and "removes our sins as far as the east is from the west?" He waits in eager anticipation to put rings on our fingers, sandals on our feet, and to gather all heaven to celebrate our return from waywardness! How often we disallow our own cleansing because we're saying to ourselves, "He can't possibly forgive me for that one again. Not again!" But every time we do that we prove our perceptions concerning Him to be wrong...again. However, while the forgiveness is immediate, many times realizing the consequences of our sin means agonizing moments waiting as a watchman for the morning—a morning that never seems to dawn upon an endless night. He makes us wait for His will to be known, that we may understand and revere His absolute omnipotence over all of life. The process of sanctification has always been about enduring faith—repentance leading to reverence, and then waiting in faith upon a holy God to see where His plan next takes us. Don't delay. Go to Him today with your sins both small and great, fearing not the marking of your iniquities. Then wait as long as it takes for the morning to break on life renewed in Christ. He will not ignore the promises He made to those who are genuinely repentant. In His timing they have already been kept, it just hasn't occurred yet in ours.

131
Finding peace in simplicity

Pray... Watch over my heart, Lord, that it may never become proud or haughty. May I never stand before You to say, "I see," but rather let me receive with meekness Your Word implanted in my mind and heart. Don't let me set my mind on great matters nor on things too profound for me. Rather, let the goal of my instruction be love from a pure heart and a good conscience and a sincere faith. Keep me from entangling myself in the everyday affairs of this world and keep my mind from the traps of meaningless speculations. Keep me also from foolish disputes over words, for these things are useless and will only harm my testimony. Calm and quiet my soul with Your abiding presence and let it be the hidden person in my heart, with the incorruptible beauty of a gentle and quiet spirit, You find precious in Your sight. Make me like a weaned child in Your presence, O God, and my soul like a weaned child within me, pursuing the things which make for peace.

O my soul, find your hope in the Lord and His government of peace that endures forever. Pursue the things that make for peace and the building up of your brothers. Do not lean upon your own understanding, but in all your ways acknowledge Him and He will direct your paths.

Consider... *Suffer hardship with me as a good soldier of Christ Jesus. No soldier in active service entangles himself in the affairs of everyday life, so that he may please the One who enlisted him as a soldier.* It is always our proud hearts that make us want to get involved in matters too great, and in things too difficult for us. It is always our pride that leads us astray from the pure simplicity of sharing the Gospel in word and deed and living in His kingdom. Hearts changed through the telling of His story will alone cause change in the only kingdom that matters to God. He cares not about earthly kingdoms, for "all the nations are as nothing before Him. They are regarded by Him as less than nothing and meaningless." Neither is He concerned for our religious freedoms, rather for our spiritual maturity which is better served by religious persecution. We cannot let the crafty one consume our attentions, rob us of our peace, and keep us from the Great Commission by letting worldly issues untrack us. If we do, we will never know the composed and quiet soul that is precious to God. Entangling ourselves in the politics and speculations inherent in the everyday affairs of this life will only bring about frustration and anger from trying to save a kingdom that does not want to be saved. Serving, sharing the good news with, and discipling one person is never too difficult for us. There is only one difference worth making, and the good soldier of Jesus Christ knows what it is: the greatest matter of all shared quietly and lovingly with one heart in need.

132

No sleep until His temple is prepared

Pray... Lord, remember me in my present trials. Consider how I have committed my life to You, confessed with my mouth and believed in my heart in Your Son, and strived to walk in Your kingdom. By Your power alive in me, I have not sought to dwell in safety, nor folded my hands to rest while others perished. Abiding in You, I have not lain down to sleep without trying to bring You glory. I have not forsaken the fellowship of the saints but endeavored to encourage my brothers in the fellowship on to love and good deeds. Bring Your Ecclesia to our knees to worship at Your feet as You arise to Your proper place in our hearts! You alone are the source of our strength, therefore clothe Your shepherds with righteousness and let Your saints shout for joy in Your presence! For the sake of Your chosen ones, do not turn Your face but walk among us and inhabit our praises. You, O Lord, have sworn in truth—You have made Your covenant with us and will not turn from it. The souls of generation after generation of those who have believed in You are secured in heaven, and if our sons will walk in faith, being careful to observe all You have taught them, they too shall never be forsaken.

You have chosen me to be one of Your holy ones and have chosen my heart to be Your eternal dwelling place. Let me therefore be diligent to prepare a resting place for You there that we might dwell together forever, for it is not Your will that any should perish. Fully provide, Lord, that I might satisfy the poor and needy with Your abundance. Clothe me with courage, discernment, and wisdom that my brothers might shout aloud for joy! Here in Your presence build up the fellowship into holy temples where Your Spirit is pleased to dwell. Knit us together in the unity of the Spirit and love, prepare a lamp for our feet, and cover our heads with the helmet of salvation. At the same time, drive our enemy out and clothe hum with shame. O God, upon Your head may Your crown forever shine!

Consider... *Be diligent to present yourselves approved to God, as workmen who do not need to be ashamed.* Oh, to live as though we knew that God had set up His very tabernacle in our hearts, and to walk as though we believed in "Christ in us, the hope of glory!" Is the world not dying to see the light? Are those dead in trespasses and sins not clamoring for the love to be made manifest when they no longer see us, but Christ in us? Have we not heard it said that we are to be His dwelling places, and our bodies living sacrifices? Oh, that His Spirit might spring forth into a dying world and a church so sorely in need of His passion! Jesus walked this earth with all the light, love, and zeal the Father is waiting to bestow upon any who will say, as He did, "Not my will be done, but Thine." Then would Jesus' prayer come true: "Thy kingdom come, Thy will be done on earth as it is in heaven!" Let us not give sleep to our eyes nor slumber to our eyelids until we have made our hearts His abode and shared His love and our bounty with others.

137

Worshipping in the midst of defeat

Pray... When the enemy rushes in to defeat me, I regret I can be weak and downcast before You, O God. When I give in to temptation and I sin, my spirit feels Your conviction and my soul becomes troubled within me. My tempter mocks when the evil desires that dwell in my flesh make me a prisoner to my former sinful desires. I step out of Your kingdom and become sin's slave. The Devil taunts me, saying "Sing now one of those worship songs in honor of Your God!" But how can I sing of Your praises in the midst of defeat and transgression? How can I worship with a heart that has grown calloused though all the battles?

Nevertheless, I cannot deny Your covenant with me and the price You paid to secure it. I cannot deny the power of this grace in which I am now privileged to stand. I cannot remove my hand from the plow and shrink back to destruction, my tongue denying You and remaining forever silent. If I denied You, where would I go and to whom would I turn, for You alone have the words of eternal life? Lord, if I did not remember Your mercy by which You saved me and Your love by which You redeemed me—if I did not steadfastly exalt You above my every desire, sin and death would win and I would be among all men most to be pitied. Oh Lord Jesus, remember me in the midst of my trials and come against the darkness that cries out, "Raze his faith! Destroy its very foundation with attacks, temptation, and deception! Remove his name forever from the Book of Life!" O, you son of lawlessness and devastation, how blessed will my God be as He repays you with the vengeance you have shown towards me. How blessed will He be as He seizes and dashes your evil plans against the holy destiny that is mine in the rock of my salvation: the Lord Jesus Christ! Amen!

Consider... *I solemnly charge you in the presence of God and of Christ Jesus to preach the Word. Be ready in season and out of season. Do not fear their intimidation, and do not be troubled. Always be ready to make a defense to everyone who asks you, to give an account for the hope that is in you.* As our sinful state fights to claim us during the trials of sanctification, and we find ourselves confronting evil, we must never forget the command to be ready in season and out...always...to make a defense of our faith. This is war, and the enemy seeks to destroy the foundations of the church so that anything built upon them will not stand. He lives to take our thoughts captive to his lies, when we should be "taking every thought captive to the obedience of Christ." But no matter the distance, all such trials are temporary for the disciple who diligently pursues the heart of God. In but a moment, with repentance as his battle-axe, the disciple charges back into the fray! It is in the midst of our trials that we truly hear the words of our blessed Savior, "I will never leave you nor forsake you." Be faithful when you sense no reward, sing in the midst of silence, rejoice in the midst of sadness, and "count it all joy when you encounter your trials...that you may be made perfect and complete, lacking in nothing." He will seize and dash Satan's evil plans against your heartfelt repentance and steadfast faith—your unwavering belief in the rock of your salvation!

139 (13-24)
Search me and know my ways

Pray... You created every cell in me, Lord. You fashioned me in my mother's womb, and I give thanks to You for I am fearfully and wonderfully made! Incredible are all Your works and my soul knows it very well. My frame was not hidden from You as I was made in secret, skillfully wrought in the depths of the earth. Your eyes alone viewed my unformed substance, and from that moment all the days that were ordained for me were written in Your book. When I had not yet lived a day, I was predestined for adoption as Your son. And how precious are Your thoughts towards me, Lord Jesus, and how vast is the sum of them! If I were to count them, they would outnumber the grains of sand under the seas. Whether I lay down or awaken I am always with You, for You forever abide in me.

Oh, that You would keep wickedness far from me, O God! Yes, depart from me, O author of deception, doubt, and fear. Get thee behind me, Satan, for you boast in pride against my God and your children take His holy name in vain. Do I not hate this one who hates You and leads Your perfect creation astray, O Lord? Do I not loathe this one who constantly prowls about, never sleeping nor slumbering, to turn the hearts of the lost, the deceived, and the naive against You? Give me a perfect hatred for him as You have given me a perfect love for You, for he has been my enemy from the beginning! Search me, O God, and know my heart—try me and know my anxious thoughts and see if there be any wicked way in me. Though at times I stumble in the way forgive me, restore me to Your kingdom, train me up in righteousness, and lead me in the everlasting way. Oh yes, continue to fill me with Your divine power, for it grants me everything pertaining to life and godliness!

Consider... *The heart is more deceitful than all else, and desperately sick. Who can understand it? I, the Lord, search the heart. I test the mind.* What a dangerous thing to say to a holy God, and yet precisely the words He longs to hear: "Search me, O God, and know my heart—try me." Do we truly seek an answer to this question, for to the extent we did I believe far more of us would learn to fear God. Do we want to suffer the wholly unknown and potentially frightful consequences of His answer? We know He is searching our hearts daily, but we try not to let it interfere with "real life." He desires that we stop keeping Him at the periphery, earnestly seek both the examination and the answer, and then have the courage to respond in faith. If we want the worker of iniquity to depart from us, we need to ask this most dangerous of all questions. "All things are open and laid bare before the eyes of Him with whom we have to do" anyway, so why try to hide? The sooner we realize He sees into our hearts whether we respond or not, ask the question, and humbly determine to walk whatever road the answer mandates, the sooner He will delight in leading us in His everlasting way.

140

Cover my head in the day of battle

Pray... Rescue me, O Lord, from the evil one. Help me discern his cunning schemes for he plans only evil. He continually stirs up warfare between my flesh and spirit, his tongue is the sharpened weapon of serpents, and the poison of deception is in his words. Make me as shrewd as he is, yet innocent as a dove as I fight this battle. Keep me, O Lord, from the clutches of wickedness and preserve me from the chaos he seeks to spread. Let me not listen to his temptations designed to trip me up. The boastful pride of life has set a hidden trap for me, and the lust of the flesh and the eyes has its cords waiting to bind me. They have spread a net for me along the path of obedience and traps for me along the righteous way. But I can always trust that You are my God—the One who hears my cries for wisdom and protection. You are my God and the cornerstone of my salvation. You cover my head in the day of battle with the helmet of discernment, You fortify my walls with truth, and clothe me with the breastplate of righteousness!

Father, I pray do not grant Satan his desires nor allow him to promote his evil schemes, for then the victory would be his. Rather, grant me the wisdom to turn away the lies he sends to deceive. In the deserts he draws me out to, let me not be anxious about my words, but rather let it be Your Spirit who speaks through me. Let me return love for evil men's hatred, and prayer for those who persecute me. Don't let their slander gain a foothold but guard my heart and mind in Christ Jesus. Then I will rest in the fact You defended my cause, as You do for all Your afflicted ones. You lift up the needy and grant justice to the poor. Having been made righteous in You, I will arise to give thanks to Your holy name. Surely, as I am made upright in You, I will live to abide in Your kingdom forever!

Consider... *You...have overcome them, because greater is He who is in you than he who is in the world.* There are two battle strategies the disciple has at the ready when confronted by evil: the ability to fight as though we knew that our battle was spiritual [not fleshly], and the power to display the peace of knowing that our eternal almighty God is greater than the temporary landlord of this world. The first allows us to see the battle with spiritual eyes, and the second brings the game to our home turf. If we fail to employ the first, we will hate the wrong enemy [our neighbor], thereby making it impossible for us to fight in the Spirit. If we fail to believe the second, the dragon of heaven will crush us, for we enter the fray with no spiritual armor. Satan schemes to surround us with the trials of our faith in an effort to get us to fight with him on his turf [in the flesh], but we must refuse. We must view the landscape with spiritual eyes, and then cry out to God, "O Lord of lords and King of kings, the strength of my salvation, cover my head in this day of battle!" He will arise, because now the fight has been entrusted to His capable hands. God will always bring justice if His afflicted ones will but approach the fight as people alive in the Spirit and dead to the flesh.

141
Listening to righteous reproof

Pray... Heavenly Father, as I call upon You may my prayer be a sweet aroma and the lifting of my hands be a worthy offering. I pray set a guard over my mouth and keep watch over the door of my lips, for how large a forest is set ablaze by the tongue's small fires? And my tongue can be a fire—the very world of iniquity You alone can tame. It is a restless evil full of deadly poison. With it I bless You, and with it I can also speak foolishly, tell lies, and curse my neighbor. Don't let my heart be enticed by evil, for it is out of the treasures of my heart my mouth will speak. Keep me also from practicing deeds of wickedness with men who love lawlessness and partake in the passing pleasures of sin. Send my righteous brothers to correct me in kindness and convict me with Your truths, for this is oil upon my head. May they not spare the rod and may I always love correction, for only fools despise wisdom and instruction. You have said that faithful are the wounds of a friend, O God, but deceitful are the kisses of the enemy.

I come against the spiritual forces of wickedness and the evil deeds they bring in my life. May their teachers be cast down at the gate that leads to heaven, while those they have deceived hear only true and righteous words from me. If the righteous do not speak, many souls will be abandoned to the tortures of hell. Keep my eyes forever focused on You, Lord. Keep my mind forever set on Your kingdom, where You dwell, and not on the things of earth. In this I know I find blessed asylum, and in Your Spirit, I will never find myself defenseless. Keep me from the jaws of the trap evil has set for me, and from the snares of the flesh that would lure me into sin. Let the wicked fall into their own nets while I pass by in safety. Guard my heart and mind in Your Son, Christ Jesus, for His nearness is my good.

Consider... *Better is open rebuke than love that is concealed. Faithful are the wounds of a friend. Reprove a wise man and he will love you.* One of the primary lessons to be learned in fellowship is trusting in our peers to first hear from God and then to guide us—be they prophet, shepherd, or lay-person. The wise realize instantly when a comrade is bringing oil for their head in the form of an admonition from above. They do not attack the messenger, nor return words of protest, for they have come to discern that correction is an integral part of discipleship, and that God works through the good word of a brother to restore them to sanity and purity. They acknowledge the author of the rebuke and love the messenger for having the courage to deliver it. 2 Samuel 16:5-13 reveals how a "heart after God's own" responds to rebuke from even the lowliest of sources. When a man turns from the faithful wounds of friends and seeks to excuse himself from the correction of the fellowship, it is a sure sign of backsliding. If we surround ourselves with those who will speak the truth in love to us, and learn to listen to God's hard lessons, we will be more able to pass through life's trials safely.

142

Pour out your complaint to God

Pray... I cry out to You, my Lord and my God! With desperation now I bring my petitions before Your throne! I pour out my complaint and voice my troubles here in Your presence, offering up my prayers and supplications to the One who alone is able to do more than I could ever think or imagine. My spirit is overwhelmed within me for my hopes deferred have made my heart sick. Help me find strength and peace in the knowledge that You know my every step and have put my tears in Your bottle. I know You have numbered the very hairs on my head, and I need not fear. And yet the powers of evil, working through my embers, have hidden traps for me everywhere. I find no one who understands to my right or to my left. There is no solution in human wisdom, and no one but You who can attend to my soul.

And so, I cry out, Lord Jesus, knowing that You are my only hope and advocate before the throne. You are the One who illuminates the darkness and my portion in the land of the living when my faith is shaken. Answer my cries, for I find myself in the depths and long to hear Your voice to bring answers to my pleas. Deliver me from the persecutions of deception, fear, chaos and temptation, for at times their influence becomes too strong for me. Even in the midst of this trap fill me to arise, in soul and in spirit, to give thanks to Your holy name! Then righteousness and peace will surround me anew because You will have dealt mercifully with me.

Consider... *But the godless in heart lay up anger. They do not cry for help when He binds them.* When we are confronted by trials that God brings or allows, we have two options: make our complaint known even at the risk of inciting His rebuke or bury it and harbor anger in our hearts. There are many of God's ways we simply will not understand in this life, for "now we see as in a mirror dimly." Trying to figure them out will lead us into frustration and even anger at times. Until I began my sojourn through the Psalms, I did not realize that the integrity Jesus desires in our relationship comes, in part, through confronting Him with our true feelings—raw, unedited words of pain that I formerly thought to be taboo. Whatever your complaint may be, He will give heed to your cry as you "work out your salvation in fear and trembling before Him." As you yearn for His fellowship in your darkest hour, your spirit is overwhelmed within you, and there is no escaping the pain, my prayer for you is that you have learned to pour out your complaint to Your God with integrity and passion through these ancient prayers. "Don't let the sun go down on your anger while giving the Devil an opportunity." Present your complaint by employing the template of the Psalms. Acknowledge the confusion that rightly comes from finite creations trying to understand and follow the commands of an infinite creator, and though your noontimes may be filled with confusion your sunsets can be peaceful ones. Shalom!

A Poem: The Prophet's Lot
(my complaint before God)

Of old, we are in the Scriptures told,
of gifts imparted through God's grace
To men to serve His bride the church,
both to build and to abase
To edify those in Him gathered—from tongues,
to administrations, to healings, to helps
Many are the gifts imparted, that
all the joints of the body may be knit together
From seasoned disciple to the new walk just started
But for me the lot cast is none of these—no, for me the road
before is beset with doubts and with burnings
With such opposed desires, a path with dangers fraught
I speak of the gift more often the curse,
I speak of the Prophet's lot
To see through His eyes such troubles,
such faults in a bride I know He, too, loves so
To be constantly availed of her travails,
yet yearning to encourage and support
To be hounded, yes rejected, by those who as shepherds
should know—by Pastors, by Priests, and time's change
To want so to fit in, to find peace with the sin,
and no longer be counted as zealous and strange
To find one I do not offend, just one with
whom to blend, a soul who would not find me contentious
Just one who would say at the dusk of our day,
"I find nothing in this man pretentious"
This is the battle that tears at our souls,
to grant comfort we cannot afford
For try as we may, those of my ilk,
we cannot escape "Thus sayeth the Lord"
Like Jonah who ran from it, Elijah who bemoaned it,

The Baptist beheaded for it, and the
Christ crucified for it, the end has always been the same
While sinners embraced them, the bride only derided,
and cast curses upon all their names
Watchmen on the walls so hopelessly anointed, ceaselessly
calling out warning and the judgments appointed
Oh, to quench for a moment the passion of
His edicts, to be content in the deceptions we see
To join with the masses as the evil time
passes in proclaiming, "It is well with me"
Nay, "Repent, for the kingdom is at hand,"
this cursed chorus of my kindred and I
Brings the mocking, the rejection, and the
anger of my lovers—the loneliness I wish here to decry
Woe is me, woe are we, the Prophets of such a zealous creed
Unyielding, unbending, though to
compromise would fulfill our every selfish need
How I envy all evangels taking the good news to the world,
while my brothers and I bring only bad to the church
All the while I desperately seek for some common ground,
but alas returning in protest to my precarious perch
How it always comes back to that for which I was begot
The lonesome voice, and the solitary
life that is the Prophet's lot
For me and my kind there can be no peace,
for our mission is one of contention
To us the greater suffering would be
to see the evil pass without struggle
And evil's will imposed without dissention
So in sum this is our lot, though I wish it were not so
How we long to express only love for the bride, but to us the
greater good is to see her grow
So we soldier on in the hope that our words will at long last
bring Jesus' laughter
Not to us, the messengers scorned,
but to His Bride revealed hereafter.

About the Psalms

As we pray through the Psalms, it is important to understand why they can literally change us from within. These poems/prayers/songs have a power that is inherent in the very purpose for which they were written: a graphic description of relationship between God and man. The following are just some of the reasons why they have the impact they do in the lives of those who regularly make them a part of their spiritual disciplines:

Written Upon the Heart

God had come to a roadblock—an obstacle that had so impeded His relationship with His people Israel that He had literally stopped caring for them (Heb. 8). Imagine that: the God of love who created His people for intimate communion with Him had become estranged from them! Something had to be done because this external, "led-by-the-hand" way wasn't working. While men could hear of Him through prophets and witness His powers through miracles, they were so disconnected from Him as to become incapable of following His commands.

And yet, in the midst of this externally-led covenant, God raised up "a man after His own heart—a man He said would *do all* of His will" (Acts 13). In an age when God led men by the hand, Psalms 40 tells us God wrote His laws upon David's heart. In this utterly unique individual, the impossible was accomplished: a Jew indwelt fully by the Holy Spirit prior to Calvary and Pentecost! Here was an Israelite who fulfilled the Great Commission of the New Covenant, in that he "observed all God commanded" under internal empowerment that was yet to come to others. What sprung from this heart after God's own was as unique as the man himself. Combining the old with the new is what David was about, so taking the Psalms and combining them with New Covenant thought, as I have endeavored to do in this work, is not such a stretch.

Jesus said what came out of the mouth begins in the heart and Paul said if we believed in our heart Jesus was Lord our salvation would be authentic. Who we are and will become begins in the heart. Everything flows from within to without, so any meaningful transformation begins within. And this is the beauty of praying the Psalms, for literally digesting God's Word by praying it can transform who we are within regardless of any external factors. Praying concerning the fear of the Lord, trials and tribulations, pain and suffering along with rejoicing and joy can all begin to become real within by praying these Psalms, and thus begin a transformation of lifestyle without as well. Bathed in the false luxuries, comforts, and securities as we are here in America, if we wish to become authentic believers, we must seek it within. That's where praying the Psalms can help.

Now God's laws are truly written upon our hearts, and His prayers can be likewise when we take advantage of the passions of David and the others who penned them by praying with them in their desperate attempts to come closer to the heart of God!

The Uniqueness of the Psalms

According to Old Testament scholars, the Psalter spans over 1,000 years of history, from Moses to Nehemiah. It is by far the longest book in the Bible and the only one with multiple scribes and five distinct sub-books. It contains both the longest and shortest chapters in the Bible, and Psalm 118:8 ["It is better to trust in the Lord, than to trust in man"] contains one of the central topics in Scripture, located in the exact center of the Scriptures.

The Psalms have withstood the test of time, and like no other book it spans the chasm between the Old and New Testaments because of the absolute and real impact it has *internally* in the heart of man. As stated before, whereas the vast majority of the books in the Bible tell us *about* God and people, the Psalms invite us into the relationship. We can actually experience all the real questions, struggles, and joys disciples of God encounters when trying to live righteously, as spiritual men, in the flesh and in a fallen world. No other book of the Bible is so uniquely positioned to draw us into its pages because of the relational nature of it.

The Psalms can literally become *our* story. We are not just invited to read them, but to become a part of the tapestry of their portrait. They are an Oasis of refreshing water from the hard rock life becomes at times. They can also play the rawest of our nerves like a finely tuned Stradivarius in the hands of a master violinist. If we internalize them by praying them, one thing they steadfastly refuse to do is to leave us unaffected, unmoved, and unconcerned when it comes to a vibrant and passionate relationship with our God, who must maintain the distance fearing Him requires, yet who bids us to reach passionately for Him *anyway*.

These songs and prayers reveal boundless joy from hearts overflowing with praise, and also desperate cries from hearts shattered by doubt and depression. But in either extreme—and everywhere in between—their profound effect on our souls comes from an intense, wholly exposed and fully experienced relationship between diligently seeking saints and a holy God. We can join them as they confront head-on their differences and rejoice in their agreements with integrity and a passion rarely witnessed in our modern world.

The Psalms as Prayers

In Psalm 72, we find these words: "The prayers of David, the son of Jesse, are ended." Psalm 90, we are told, is a "prayer of Moses." Songs and prayers go hand-in-hand in the Psalms. They are the cries of men's hearts to God for answers, communion, and relationship. They are requests to extend the soul and spirit beyond the point of merely knowing Him to more fully *experiencing* Him. What sprung from this heart after God's own was a book that can transform the very soul of any person who will but connect through prayer to them.

Worship and prayer are how man's spirit communes intimately with God. As we enter in, we seek a deeper level of communication with Him than mere study or teaching will ever take us. We do not pray and worship to talk *at* God, but rather to be *with* Him. It is here we seek to engage our emotions and our hearts, as well as our minds, in our quest to abide with Him more fully.

In his book *Postmodern Pilgrims,* Leonard Sweet says this of what it is today's worshippers, frustrated with the modern church, look for:

"For the church to incarnate the Gospel in this postmodern world, it must become more medieval than modern, more apostolic than patristic. I call postmodernity an EPIC culture: Experiential, Participatory, Image-driven and Connected... Western Christianity went to sleep in a modern world governed by the gods of reason and observation. It is awakening to a postmodern world open to revelation, and hungry for experience."

True followers of Jesus crave an "experiential, participatory, image-driven, and connected relationship" with the God of their salvation. They desire a wholistic relationship: body, mind, heart, soul, and spirit with God. People know intuitively that prayer is the place this relationship with Christ should be forming, because prayer is where they should be communicating most intimately with Him. We witness Christ's relationship with His Father, a relationship bathed in His prayers, and know that this is the model of the relationship He seeks with all His children in prayer. Yet, most Christians [men particularly] struggle desperately to find it. I believe this because I've talked to so many about it as I have shared my story with them.

Making the Connection

We have made prayer a head thing when it's not. We try to reach the Gates of Heaven on the wings of knowledge, through formulas we've been led to believe will lead us to an effective connection. As I say in my book, *The Kingdom Election*, knowledge is the language of religion while revelation is the language of the kingdom. Knowledge based prayers emanate from our minds, instead of heartfelt cries for connection founded in the communion of God's Spirit with ours. We don't need to become proficient in the doctrine of prayer, employ man's formulas, or have considerable knowledge on the subject to enter into a deep and meaningful experience. In fact, that most often just gets in the way.

In our struggle to connect through mental means, we are confronted by these words in Romans 8, "The Spirit also helps our weakness, *for we do not know how to pray as we should*, but the Spirit Himself intercedes for us with groanings too deep for words. And He who searches the hearts knows what the mind of the Spirit is, because He intercedes for the saints according to the will of God." Here it is in black and white: we don't know how to pray as we should. When Jesus' disciples asked Him how to pray, He responded, "Pray then in this way" and then proceeded to give them what we now call The Lord's Prayer. Why didn't

He just say, "Pray whatever comes to your mind... whatever is on your heart?"

When you think about it, in light of Romans 8, Jesus' answer makes perfect sense. He knew men didn't know how to pray employing merely mental approaches, so He gave them words to pray from His own lips. They were words prayed according to the Spirit and therefore *had* to be according to the will of God. Prayer is about the connection of our spirit [the spirit of man] with the Holy Spirit [the Spirit of God]. To pray with the heart of Jesus and His Spirit, as the Psalmists did, we simply need to follow their lead as Jesus instructed His disciples to follow His lead.

We inevitably fail to connect when we go to our heavenly Father with only what is on our *minds,* or a prepared list of what we want and try to pray meaningful prayers. To pray from mere knowledge inevitably results in hopelessly wandering thoughts and shallow expression. I spent years in this state of futility, distanced from God in my prayer life, as I tried to pray what was on my mind. Until I started praying the Psalms, I didn't realize there were 150 or more "Lord's Prayers" to be found there!

As is true in all things, "what is impossible for man has been made possible by God," because He's already given us prayers that are *according to His will.* If we pray with the prayers He's given us, He has said His Spirit will be there to intercede for us. He connects directly with our spirits as we join in *His* prayers, His Spirit searches our hearts and also knows His mind and His will, and the blessed connection can be made!

What we find in the Psalms are prayers from the Spirit that can lead anyone who prays them regularly into the fulfilling *groanings* Romans alludes to. They form vivid word pictures, much as Jesus did through the use of His parables, that lead us to a deeper, more connected plane of communication. It is a realm simply not possible for the mind of man apart from God's intercession.

Prayer's Highest Calling

The prayers of the Psalms, surprisingly, are rarely intercessory in nature. For the most part they involve two players: God and the participant. But doesn't that make perfect sense, inasmuch as prayer was designed ultimately around relationship? While certainly we find prayers interceding for nations in the Psalms, even those prayers are aimed more at the writer's involvement as a part of the process.

The benefits of interceding for others are certainly abundant in the Scriptures, and God gifts many with the gift of intercession, but even the effectiveness of everything we undertake for others springs from our foundational relationship with Him. The primary reason for prayer must be a two-way communication between the Creator and the created, for if we don't get that one right the entire house of prayer is constructed upon sand.

I have found through my personal journey in these prayers an inescapable transformation takes place in the soul [see chapter: Inescapable Callings]. Reading the Psalms is a good thing to do, but we can easily store learning in our already over-stuffed warehouses of knowledge and miss out on the *experience*, passion, integrity, reverence, and relationship that is there to be had through digesting them in prayer. When we personalize and internalize those same words by praying them, we find a pervasive passion that cannot be ignored nor escaped fully capable of transforming us from the inside out, as all things from the Spirit of God do. His Word comes to abide deeply in our hearts and minds, and we in it.

If made a regular practice, praying the Psalms can literally change us from modernized religious observers to the medieval, apostolic disciples! It can bring about a metamorphosis that comes in the form of taking knowledge and transforming it into experience and revelation. You cannot immerse your soul in the sometimes calm and serene—sometimes tumultuous and raging seas—of the Psalms and remain passively spectating on the sidelines of a superficial relationship with God. You cannot immerse your soul in the graphic and titanic spiritual warfare that permeates the Psalms, and remain in those "safe places" the church promotes from which to sit and observe the great adventure you should be participating in.

The Psalms call you out of your comfortable seat on the bleachers and into the competition between light and darkness desperately raging for your soul. Fully partaking in the Psalms, through praying them, transports us from being "held by His hand" to having His very life "written upon our hearts" (Heb. 8). So, engage and connect!

Specific New Testament changes:

Some of the areas impacted by engaging the New Covenant in God's ancient prayers I alluded to in the Introduction are as follows:

The enemy's new clothes: As I began praying through the Psalms, I found my biggest roadblock came in the form of how to handle the Psalmist's many references dealing with flesh and blood enemies. Jesus said we are to love our enemies and pray for those who persecute us (Matt. 5). Yet, I came repeatedly upon verses that spoke of the hatred for, and destruction of, fleshly foes. I struggled mightily with this dilemma, until during my meditations the Spirit opened my eyes to the answer in Ephesians 6, where Paul says our struggle is not against flesh and blood but against principalities, powers, and rulers of darkness and wickedness in the heavenly places.

There is an enemy we all face as believers, the same one who has sought to pervert and destroy everything God cherishes down through the ages. He incited David's earthly enemies to hate him and engages us in a conflict today every bit as critical to spiritual welfare as any battle David ever faced defending country and throne.

As long as Satan is allowed to roam this earth and deceive the faithful, we will never be without a real and wicked foe to conquer and a life-hangs-in-the-balance battle to fight. This warfare we are engaged in is more a life-and-death struggle than the ones David ever faced, because the consequences are eternal. One is not called to wear the full armor of God to a tea party!

It is no offense to the New Covenant to pray against Satan and his dark minions with all the passion and fervor the Psalmists intended towards their earthly enemies. The revelation of this gave me the answer I had sought for! I could transform the Psalmist's struggles with earthly foes, who sought to destroy their flesh, into my struggle with principalities and powers of darkness that now seek to destroy my soul.

Armed to fight the good spiritual fight, the Psalms help us become far more able to deftly engage the enemy. If we take the attributes and characteristics that the Psalmists ascribe to their earthly foes and ascribe them to our spiritual ones, we can identify them, remove the gloves, and go on the offensive!

A new kingdom: In Old Covenant times, there was but one kingdom available to us: the kingdom of man. Then Jesus came heralding a starkly contrasting kingdom with the most important nine words ever spoken [see my book, The Kingdom Election available on Amazon], "Repent for the kingdom of heaven is at hand!" Now the believer has two separate and distinct kingdoms from which to choose and to declare their citizenship, not one.

There is no more important message we grasp, believe, and engage in than this reality of a literal kingdom of heaven on earth! It was the announcement that heralded Jesus' coming to earth, the one He preached first and most about, the first request of His most famous prayer, the one eleven of the parables start with, and the specific gospel He is recorded as preaching and modeling.

During a period He called "the birth pangs" that would precede His second coming, Jesus said "the gospel of the kingdom would be preached throughout the world" (Matt. 24) and I believe these are the days we are living in. He said the two kingdoms arising against each other in great power would mark this period, and I believe there is no decision we can make that will determine our earthly and eternal destiny more than which kingdom we elect to become citizens of. Because of its critical importance, you will find references to this new kingdom and what it means throughout this devotional.

The name of Jesus: Another must in engaging the New Covenant is to enlist the name of Jesus Christ in the prayers. While the Psalmists made references to Christ, He is for obvious reasons never mentioned by name. However, when we realize Christ was the Word made flesh, who dwelt among us and existed since the beginning with God as the Alpha and Omega (John 1), how could He not be all of God's Word, both New Testament and Old?

It is to Jesus Christ, through whom we have been granted access to the throne of grace and gained access to God's presence with our petitions that we pray. It is also in His name we are told to pray (Rom. 15, Phil. 1) and He who "lives to make intercession" for us before the Father.

Geography: universal vs. specific: There are several references made in the Psalter to specific geographical points of reference that held spiritual significance in the Old Testament. They do not hold such meaning under the New Covenant's more universal approach to the boundlessness of God's new kingdom on earth. His new chosen ones are now grafted into the faith from all corners of the globe, all cultures, and all walks of life. I have therefore used terms such as, "the whole world...all creation...His church... all Your people...believers everywhere," etc., in the stead of confined geographical boundaries used by the Psalmists.

Empowerment [internal vs. external]: The working of the Holy Spirit takes on a meaning to disciples of Jesus known to precious few in Old Covenant times. With the lone exception of David's claim God's laws were within His heart, echoing the mark of the New Covenant in Hebrews 8, the Psalms lack references to His indwelling empowerment not made widely available until Jesus paid the price for sin. In the Old Testament, motivation was of the external, "led-by-the-hand" variety (Heb. 8). We now live under an internal covenant, where the power to be righteous comes only through Christ's righteousness imparted to us through His SpiritoHHThere T, and we no longer rely upon our own righteousness.

Many references exist in the Psalms to men walking in their own righteousness and operating under their own power. Through statements like these the failure of the Old Covenant, due to the impossibility of men being good enough, becomes apparent. I have altered these into requests that God, through His Holy Spirit that now indwells us, would "help... let...empower...bid us...and fill us" to be able to be obedient and walk in His righteousness, not our own.

Grace and security: While there are many references to God's lovingkindnesses towards His often-rebellious people in the Psalms, the concept of grace in a New Covenant context is understandably missing. Although I find as much evidence of grace in the Old Testament as in the New, I have altered Old Covenant ideas that concern grace for this reason. While I am of the opinion the eternal security debate is not as cut and dried as those on either side of the isle contend it is, the statements made by the Psalmists often portray a rigidity that offends any orthodox view of New Covenant grace.

No more promises: The Old Covenant was based upon men keeping God's commandments, and that is at least to some extent the reason for its failure. Men pursued by their sinful natures were then, and are now, incapable of keeping promises. Promises made and not kept become lies and lies are sin. Jesus said, "You have heard that the ancients [OC] were told, 'You shall not make false vows, but shall fulfill your vows to the Lord.' But Jesus said [NC], "Make no oath at all, either by heaven for it is the throne of God, or by the earth for it is the footstool of His feet...But let your statement be, 'yes, yes' or 'no, no.' Anything beyond these is of *evil*" (Matt. 5). James 5 echoes this very sentiment. Even under the old way Solomon chimes in, "It is better that you should not vow than that you should vow and not pay" (Eccl. 5).

The Psalms are veritably laced with men making promises to God, and therefore I have replaced these promises with requests for God to help us be men whose "Yes is yes, and no, no" through the power of His Spirit and our obedience.

A new battlefront: In the Psalms, there is much said about men of violence fighting battles in the flesh over earthly real estate, for the kingdom of God at that time was a physical kingdom. Home base was a physical location and the way to defend it was through physical conflict with other people trying to take it away.

But the kingdom of heaven on earth is a spiritual one and home base is the Holy Spirit living within us, as God's new temples (1 Cor. 3). We defend it through weapons described as "the shield of faith, the helmet of salvation, and the sword of the Spirit" (Eph. 6) imparted to us as gifts of faith from God. Passages in the Psalms that speak of such battles have therefore been modified to reflect the temptations and deceptions of our spiritual enemy aimed squarely at our souls.

Satan's attacks upon our faith are far more dangerous than physical oppression, one being eternal and the other temporal, and therefore these physical circumstances I have transformed to target doctrines that come against the truth and cause deception. Jesus said of the differences of these attacks, "Do not fear those who kill the body, but are unable to kill the soul. But rather fear Him who is able to destroy both soul and body in hell" (Matt. 10).

There is no amount of physical persecution that can sway one who is solidly grounded spiritually, so Satan has turned his big guns to deceive and tempt on us. This is especially true in our American version of Christianity that has not known the slightest sort of physical persecution in a very long time. Our fight is with deception and, unfortunately, there is nowhere spiritual deception finds more fertile ground than where there is no physical oppression. That is why coming to understand spiritual warfare through the lens of its physical counterparts in the Psalms can be such a valuable tool to us here in our Laodicean church environment.

Personalizing the Psalms: Many of the Psalms are not written in a first-person format. Therefore, where there are references to God as "He...His," I have altered many of these to say, "You...Yours," etc. There are many other areas where the tense has been changed to help the readers to personalize the prayers so that they flow easily from them to God as an intimate conversation. An exception to this is the many instances where the Psalmists command their own souls, saying, "O my soul, praise Him," etc. It is a lost art, and one we need to reinstate, this idea of commanding our own souls to obedience and worship.

I fully believe you will experience the inescapable callings of the Psalms as you make praying them a regular part of your daily meditations. I am convinced, after many years of immersing myself in them, there is no greater personal practice that has been given to us for the purpose of enhancing communion between earthly beings and their heavenly Creator than praying God's own words along with, and back to, Him. Do this regularly, and it can transform you from the inside out!

Inescapable Callings of the Psalms

Praying the Psalms, if made a regular practice, opens the door to inescapable callings in our souls. Through the miraculous power of the Holy Spirit praying God's own words with and through us, these callings sink deeply into our "inner man." They can literally "write His laws upon our hearts." The door opens to them indwelling us, becoming a part of us, and affecting everything we do, say, and think.

But to reap those rewards, one must be willing to enter in with determination and resolve, desiring to earnestly and diligently pursue transformation. Generations of ascetics in monasteries around the world have made praying the Psalms a daily and crucial part of their devotionals, because they know in their spirits the following characteristics are constantly recurring themes that become pervasive and inescapable soul-transformers to those willing to engage:

The Warfare

Dr. Larry Crabb has this to say about the nature of the fight we are in with the enemy, whether we like it or not in his book *Connecting*:

> The flesh, the enemy within, dons a friendly uniform—one that a Christian might wear, and suggests reasonable directions. We welcome him into our ranks...When what we need to do, of course, is shoot him. Naïve Christians...do not want to enter the battle raging in their souls...Spiritual warfare, they hope, will involve only light skirmishes, never a fight-till-someone-dies conflict.[i]

This is war! This battle with Laodicean lukewarmth and complacency is actually more of a life-and-death issue than the defense of his nation was to David. The consequences of failure are more severe than any conceivable physical battle because they are eternal. This is not a conflict that will involve only light skirmishes, just because it is not physically life-threatening.

Jesus' judgment on the Laodiceans for being lukewarm were the most severe of any of the churches He rebuked. In Old Testament times, God leveled a similar judgment against the Jews, that He would "search Jerusalem with lamps and punish the men who were stagnant in spirit—who said in their hearts, 'The Lord will not do good or evil'" (Zeph. 1).

The dangers we face dealing with Satan are not found in the wounds we will take while fighting him, but in the numbness we become vulnerable to while being deceived into complacently ignoring him. While we should not spend inordinate amounts of time focusing on the evil one, we should always be wary of his absolute and never-ending fealty to the cause of our destruction. That means the constant need for awareness, discernment, and employing the shrewdness of a serpent when dealing with him.

And do we ever stop to think that our image of Satan's powers and abilities is proportionately tied to our image of those attributes of God? Do we consider that to the extent our image of a righteous, just, to-be-feared and holy God becomes watered down, our image of an equally evil, deceptive, to-be-respected and merciless enemy likewise becomes distorted? When this happens, life becomes a never-ending monotonous soup of false and unexciting perceptions—a condition that, by definition, is the lukewarmth Jesus condemned in the Laodiceans. We lose discernment and clarity when we fall into superficiality, unable to eat the solid food God has for the mature (Heb. 5). Our senses remain unable to discern either good [God] or evil [Satan], and we become defenseless babes when the Serpent whispers in our ear, "Has God said?"

If there is one thing David understood it was warfare, both physical and spiritual. He used a tool we should consider employing today, and that was to command his soul to do his bidding. Spiritual warfare takes place among the tripart members of man: spirit, soul, and flesh. The soul—our mind, will, and emotions—stands in-between the spirit and the flesh, receiving input and beckonings from both. If it receives, embraces, and follows the flesh then the deeds of the flesh, ungodliness, and carnal living will result. If, on the other hand, our soul pays heed to and follows the spirit, which is in direct contact with God's Spirit godliness, righteousness, and peace will result. We literally take on "the mind of Christ" (1 Cor. 2).

By commanding his soul David is literally taking dominion over His thought life and thus his flesh. He is saying, "Be advised O mind, will, and emotions that my spirit is in charge here and is commanding you to line up with what God desires, not what you want!" When we feel temptation knocking at the door this is a good practice to employ because it reminds us:

- The battle for the kingdom, righteousness, and our very salvation is fought in the soul
- Spiritual warfare is indeed real and happening,
- We need to enter in and engage,
- We need to hear from the Holy Spirit to discern good and evil,

- Our spirit, hearing from His Spirit, needs to be the one in charge,
- Greater is the One in us than the one who commands the worldly.

If we look into who was motivating David's enemies, praying the Psalms brings us into the experience of spiritual warfare and helps us to identify the enemy in all of his various disguises. They paint a portrait of Satan as the vilest of creatures: beautiful in disguise, tenacious in resolve, treacherous in heart, and dedicated to our destruction through deception.

The Psalms are fairly dripping with tales of vanquishing the enemy, persecution for righteousness' sake, good versus evil, right versus wrong, and darkness versus light. They vividly display the hearts of determined men of faith intimately acquainted with grief, yet full of passion—people caught up in a desperate quest to engage in, and win, their battles. Praying the Psalms brings to our doorstep an acute sense of spiritual warfare by graphically defining both our Advocate and our enemy, and what men of action and faith do to prevail!

The Reverence

Dallas Willard describes what ails the church today concerning the loss of a healthy fear of God in his book, The Divine Conspiracy:

> What lies at the heart of the astonishing disregard of Jesus found in the moment-to-moment existence of multitudes of professing Christians is a simple lack of respect for Him.[ii]

An accurate portrayal of the healthy fear of God is a primary and recurring theme throughout the Psalms. It is one I believe is tied very closely to the issue of passion lost. There are approximately 45 verses in the Psalms that refer to the benefits of embracing this respect. Ironically, they contain every good and wonderful promise in all of Scripture [see appendage: The promises of God to those who fear Him]. There is not a benefit God offers that is not to be found there: including both new and old testament doctrines.

What does it mean to fear the Lord? Through the prophet Malachi God poses this question: "A son honors his father and a servant his master. Then if I am a father, where is My honor? And if I am a master, where is My respect" (Mal. 1)? The fear of the Lord can be defined as ultimate respect, total awe, and complete reverence for the otherness of the King of all creation—a respect given no other dream, desire, person, or object. There exists a distance even a loving God must maintain between Himself and His created beings that is absolute, unknowable, uncanny, and inscrutable to them. It is the chasm that reassures creation God will remain God and what is created will never be able to supplant Him. It was a distance Lucifer tried to bridge and suffered eternal consequences. While we are on this earth, and even after, there will be a majesty, a soul, a character, and a power belonging to God that we will in our finest moments view only "as in a mirror dimly."

While it's true the God of all mercies reached down from heaven, emptied Himself, and came in the form of man to restore intimate relationship with us, we must never forget that He is also the God who came to judge the world (John 5). Isaiah 55 records, "His thoughts and ways are as high above ours as the heavens are above the earth." Yes, "we have the mind of Christ" (1 Cor. 2), but that does not make us God. Yes, He brought the very heavens to earth, but nonetheless the limitations of flesh and sin inhibit its fulness.

Acknowledging and deeply respecting the fact that, while He loves us and His Spirit indwells us, He is still *other* than us—an otherness that in our finest moments we cannot begin to penetrate—is what fear of the Lord is. It was David's constant quest to penetrate that otherness regardless of his many flaws. It gave him an insight into fearing God that can enlighten us when joining his prayers in the Psalms. We can realize our vulnerability to the desires of our flesh, and still lift desperate cries for nearness to the impenetrable otherness of a holy God.

And the calls to fear God are by no means limited to the Old Testament. In the New Testament it is written:

- We are to offer to God acceptable service, with reverence and awe, because He is a consuming fire (Heb. 12),
- Knowing the fear of the Lord, we are to persuade men (2 Cor. 5),
- We are to cleanse ourselves from all defilements, and perfect holiness in this holy fear (2 Cor. 7),
- We are to be subject to one another in the fear of Christ (Eph. 5),
- We are to work out our salvation with fear and trembling (Phil. 2),
- We are to conduct ourselves in fear during our time on earth (1 Pet. 1).

In the end, the saints gathered around the throne will hear a great angel proclaiming, "Fear God, and give Him glory, because the hour of His judgment has come" (Rev. 14)! He is both Lamb and Lion, Savior and Judge, and we will never understand Him embracing the watered-down teachings of religion that ignore the Lion and the Judge and worship only the god of love and mercy.

The prophet Isaiah said Jesus, the One who brings mercy, love and forgiveness, would come with "the Spirit of the Lord resting upon Him—the spirit of wisdom and understanding, counsel and strength, knowledge, and the fear of the Lord," and that Jesus Himself would "delight in the fear of the Lord" (Isa. 11). This had to be so because He came to us as a man and "was tempted in all things as are we" (Heb. 4) while with us. Jesus said we were not to be afraid of those who can only kill the flesh, but rather warned us to fear the One whom He feared and had the sole authority to both kill the body and cast the soul into hell (Luke 12). He said this while talking to His "friends," a term He used to describe those closest to Him.

Furthermore, fearing God does not stop with the Father because the lineage of judgment did not end with the Father. The very One religion ascribes only grace and love to is the very One who, with fire in His eyes, will judge all of us! John tells us that the Father no longer judges anyone, but that He has given all judgment to Jesus because He desires that we all would honor [fear] Jesus (John 5). Judgment did not cease when the new replaced the old, it was rather passed from the Father to the capable hands of the Son because He uniquely had experienced both the divinity and humanity, had overcome the world, and reconciled God and man and heaven and earth.

So, before we think we've divorced ourselves from a fearful God through the unbalanced emphasis upon grace religion teaches today, perhaps we'd best review our picture of the One we attribute that grace to. We might want to find out how He feels about it before we get to feeling too comfortable with a concept of grace that is more of our making than His.

If we feared God we would find in Him far more depth, more to adore, more wonder, and more warrior and King to ignite our passions! If we feared God, we would stop putting Him in a prettily wrapped box called "grace and mercy," which holds little inside to capture our passions and we would set Him in a chariot with wheels of fire! The fear of the Lord simply must be embraced if we want to enter His kingdom and become people after God's own heart once again.

Fearing God is the only way a human heart after God's approaches the heart that is God's with a proper balance of adoration and respect, and therefore is such a popular theme in the Psalms. One cannot pray the Psalms regularly and fail to come to a proper understanding and appreciation of this healthy fear of God. One cannot come to a new appreciation of His otherness and not kindle anew the fires of passion!

The Integrity

Relationships must contain certain basic elements if they are to transcend mere acquaintance. One of the primary characteristics both parties of a healthy relationship must display is integrity. How many people do we become friends with who are disingenuous, or whom we don't feel we can trust? How close do we get to someone with whom we can't carry on anything but the most superficial of conversations because we don't trust them with our inner thoughts? Likewise, how many of our true friends consistently approach us in the same superficial way, regardless of how we may have treated each other, our moods, or our circumstances?

This begs the question as to why we often try to build a relationship with God through often disingenuous, repetitive, and superficial conversations in prayer? When we approach our true friends and we're angry, do we not tell them? If they are doing something we don't understand that is hurting us or those we love, do we not question? If some demand they made upon our life was unclear or confusing, would we not seek clarity? If someone we counted upon seemed to be conspicuously missing in our hour of need, would we not voice our protest? Of course, we would!

Why then do we go to throne room of God, who knows our own thoughts and hearts better than our closest friends—who knows His plans for us are sometimes confusing and our anger and protest may be warranted—with superficial requests, shallow demeanor, and dutiful but insincere praise? This is the kind of superficiality we cannot possibly build human relationships upon, and yet we hope to build a relationship with God upon the same foundation? Relationship is what He created us for and what He sent His Son to restore. He has fully done His part by dealing with the sin that separated us from Him and infusing us with the Holy Spirit who came to be the communicator/interpreter between us.

The Psalmists were brutally honest with their Maker and it led them into a fuller, richer, more intimate relationship with Him than most of us experience today. It is not God's fault we fail to reach a depth with Him that is ultimately satisfying to both parties. He is fully able to take us into intimacy we cannot imagine. He is fully transparent, unimaginably deep, always true, and never lacking in consistency and integrity. The shortcomings are ours and we owe it to ourselves to do all possible to come near to Him as possible. In the Psalms David says, "But as for me, the nearness of God is my good" (Ps. 73) and he did everything possible to find and keep that nearness.

Did Jesus spare His heavenly Father integrity when He cried out "My God, my God, why hast Thou forsaken me?" Then why do we think this same Jesus would expect rosy, pious reports or canned, pre-packaged presentations from us every time we speak to Him? In prayer, more than anywhere else, He desires honesty from us. Our Savior was a wild and woolly maverick, unafraid to talk mano-a-mano any time anyone wanted to belly up to the bar! He welcomes that same integrity when we come to Him in prayer—the integrity we find so uncensored in the Psalms.

When we build a relationship upon a foundation of integrity, we begin to bring God into more of life. We're less ashamed to approach Him with our struggles with the flesh, or to confront Him when were frustrated with the otherness that must to an extent cause distance and questioning, so we invite Him into places we never would have considered inviting Him into before and we get answers to questions we never would have even asked before. We begin to "pray without ceasing" (1 Thess. 5), because we realize that all the circumstances and trials of life—the good, the bad, and the mundane—are issues we can openly and candidly discuss with Him. We realize that our prayer relationship is building every minute of every day, and there is nothing that is "off the table" as our imperfections confront His perfection.

There is no better place to develop integrity than joining those who suffered through their stories of life with brutal candor before a holy God in the Psalms.

These are just some of the many benefits we will find in returning to an ancient practice once commonly held by God's people, through "speaking to one another in songs, and hymns, and spiritual songs" (Eph 5). To reach the very heart of God and maintain a vital and alive relationship full of passion and reverence, there is no byway around understanding spiritual warfare, holy fear, and integrity.

These characteristics, and many more to ignite the soul, are to be found in abundance following the prayer highway to Jesus' awaiting heart constructed so masterfully in the Psalms. Its inescapable callings are so palpable and ultimately so desirable they invite all who will engage to conquer the shallowness of life we all confront in the comforts of the flesh the kingdom of man constantly serves up to untrack our attentions. They lure us into a sometimes uncomfortably real and yet oh, so fulfilling a relationship with our Creator, along with a spiritual walk here on this earth we perhaps never thought possible.

The Passion

Why did God select David: a man fraught with insecurities and lustful desires—a man He knew would commit adultery and then deceive and even murder a loyal servant—to reside over the golden age of Israel? Why would He likewise select Peter: a man with an impetuous, overbearing, and I'm sure offensive personality to many to entrust the keys to the kingdom of heaven to? After all there was John, "the disciple whom Jesus loved," and certainly tamer men than David in his day to bestow these honors upon. If we are to be known by our love, and if love is the greatest gift, then why not select less hard-edged men than David and Peter?

Despite their failings, these two were men of unbridled passion! When it concerns nurturing, the lot might best fall to lovers like John. When it comes to teaching, the lot might fall to those more intelligent and understanding: a Paul or perhaps a Luke. But when ushering in new eras for His people is the goal, where that not seen must supplant that which has been seen, the lot falls to fearless trailblazers—to men of *passion*!

In spite of all their failings, David and Peter confronted life and their relationship with its Giver with great zeal. When they were knocked down through trial from above, attacks from below, or failings from within they got up, repented, dusted themselves off and then charged boldly into the fray again! They clung like starved Gila-monsters to the impenetrable otherness of a God who bid them come to the fore of the battle with laser-like focus and courage, ready to sacrifice all for the glory of an as-yet uncertain kingdom.

And here's one of the foremost reasons we need men regularly praying the Psalms today: the modern church is confronted with a profound *lack* of passion in her men. We see this in the apathetic posture the vast majority of them now display towards all things spiritual. David and Peter may have been many unsavory things, but apathetic and lazy they were not. The passion we see displayed in these two cornerstones of the faith has not died any more so than the Spirit that still indwells men has somehow changed. It has merely been buried under too many years of the lack of passion that is historically inherent in the unbridled freedom, wealth, and security we've enjoyed for far too long here in America. While these may appear beneficial to the worldly, they are dangerous influences for the Sons of Adam who have been cursed since the Garden of Eden with apathy, laziness, and abandonment of their posts.

We are passion-challenged in the modern church because we simply have not suffered for many, many years, and in the Greek definition of passion an element of suffering is necessary. On the contrary, we have made an art form of doing everything possible to avoid suffering. When man knows no real suffering, he forfeits many of his chances to engender passion. When living in a society where everything is a mouse-click or five-minute drive away—a society rich in earthly securities and abundance—passion is slowly drained away and false and dangerous feelings of well-being rule.

The sort of passion David and Peter knew must be proactively sought out here in the streets of Laodicea if it is to be found. We must deliberately put ourselves in harm's way for the sake of the Gospel. According to Paul, the One who came to free us from the law left us with a law of His own: "to bear one another's burdens and so fulfill *the law* of Christ" (Gal. 6). This *requires* we "offer our bodies as living, holy sacrifices" (Rom. 12), physically as well as spiritually putting ourselves in harm's way for the sake of others. It *requires* that we move from the safety of our side of the road and into life's gutters that are only to be found on that side of the road we wouldn't naturally travel. Stepping into the suffering of others can be the elixir when our own passionless lives know precious little of it.

Spiritually, we find great suffering in the life of David. He endured many injustices at the hands of Saul, Israel's enemies, and even his own family. Here was a man informed of his divine anointing from the time he was a boy yet was found hiding in caves and estranged from the people it was prophesied he would lead when he had grown. David's resolve to follow God, however, never allowed him to give up and the passion that resulted coursed through every fiber of his being. We must knock diligently and hard on the door of passion—as David did—if we are to have it opened to us. It will not be ours through comfortable church attendance and Bible studies.

This brings a final element in the quest for passion into focus, and that is endurance. For my money, the most complete promise in all of Scripture is found in James 1, "And let endurance have its perfect result that you may be perfect and complete, lacking in nothing." This is the very same word Jesus uses when He commands, "Be *perfect* as your Heavenly Father is perfect." Kingdom perfection is found in a race well run and finished—in a process of increasing faith, not necessarily in victory or defeat. Those who wish to know passion must be enduring men of extraordinary faith because suffering requires perseverance through trials and perfection will not be reached without it.

We can escape this passionless, bland existence in America, and seek the closeness to God passionate men knew if we will but start by putting ourselves spiritually into their place in prayer. That cannot help but lead to physically entering into harm's way through being good Samaritans and endure it all with peace and joy.

We *can* get this close to God in prayer, but we must risk the danger of coming so close to Jesus that we actually touch Him and join in His sufferings for the sake of others. Jesus, another passionate guy who knew much suffering, yes? Are you willing to pay the price to know His suffering and feel His unbridled passion? Praying the Psalms offers us all an opportunity like few others to get this close, but as with all things concerning Jesus physical obedience and spiritual growth go hand-in-hand. Praying the Psalms offers us a way to know intimately and with full connectedness the passion of saints. Though our Laodicean environment works hard to deny us this connection, when we step into David's world it's game on!

Praying the Psalms can help awaken us from the fog comfort draws us into. Praying the Psalms can bring us inescapably back into the passion of its scribes. Praying the Psalms can plunge us headlong into the fight-to-the-death warfare that rages daily for our souls. Praying the Psalms can place us in dark caves fearing for our lives, and onto a battlefield full of life and death. Praying the Psalms can draw us back into understanding suffering and thus back to passion.

Epilogue

The work of writing does not come in the creation of words, for that is the domain of the joy of writing. The work is encountered in the endless editing and re-writing that inevitably follows the joys. Pouring over that just-finished manuscript to see prose you penned just months, weeks, even days before, now crying out for minor and even major surgery, is the bane of an author's existence. It is an exhausting endeavor, yet unfortunately we must look at our prized creation with a discerning eye and work and rework it again until it is as right as we know how to make it. When we are finished with it, we then confront editors who wish to engage in the whole sordid business all over again. That side of it cannot be ignored if we want our creation to reach into the heart of the reader and provide a benefit to them, for it is the way of love to see what God has inspired within us done with excellence before it is shared with others.

It is at the end of the journey, long after the creative juices have simmered and the editing is done, that we can finally rest and go to press. Upon initially finishing these devotionals [first written in the

1990's] I wanted to put it all aside for a while as I had done with prior finished works. I wanted to go on to those "new things" God is always doing that would give insight into new perspectives and the joys of creating again after being so thoroughly immersed in this one for so long. The last thing I typically want to do after finishing a project is to go back and re-visit it. I need a vacation, a breather, a break from the object of my desire that has for so long been the landlord of my thoughts. But it was not to be so with these ancient prayers.

It is the highest testimony I could give that short-ly after putting them aside I found I was inextricably drawn back to joining my heart to God through the hearts of the Psalmists in prayer. In such a pitifully brief time I had become like a parched wanderer in a smoldering desert, my old nemesis Minduscon-stantwanderitis was back with a vengeance, and I was lost once again in the wilderness of my own men-tal prayers. I knew I needed to return to drink deeply at my oasis of passion, integrity, and fervency that I realized I could find nowhere but praying the words of God. Romans 8 resounded with truth and life, as I was finally and fully convinced that I had no clue "how to pray as I should." I needed the Spirit of God to intercede for me again, through His words and ac-cording to His will, and not my own.

I surrendered in that moment, realizing I was gladly and joyfully hooked! I had become a Psalm-praying junkie who would need his regular fix to survive for as long as I lived. It was time to come out of the closet and admit it. And that's precisely why I know this thing is from the Spirit. Even after the tedious work of considering and reconsidering, editing and re-editing, and designing and re-designing, the power and the Spirit breaks through anew every time I drink deeply from the life-giving springs of the Psalms! Every time I come back to them it is like a mighty wave of intimacy and connection with His kingdom rolling over me.

With the dawning of each day, I can begin another journey through the Psalter and it's always as fresh and new as it was when I first began. But that's what sets the Word of God apart from all pretenders, isn't it? That newness and freshness the Spirit brings to it as He, the Father, and the Son hook up in us to reveal His marvelous truths and grant us revelation cannot be found in the words of any lesser god!

The Psalms: The promises of God to those who fear Him

15:1-4 – The character, integrity and selflessness of those who fear God

19:9 – The purity and enduring quality of a fear of God

25:14 – God reveals His secrets to those who fear Him, making known His covenant

31:19 – He stores up goodness for those who fear Him

33:18 – His eye is upon them

34:7 – His angels encamp around them, to rescue them

34:9 – For those who fear Him, there is no want

36:1 – Transgression and ungodliness is in the hearts of those who do not

55:19-20 – He puts forth His hand against those who do not

60:4 – He gives a banner of truth to those who fear Him

64:9 – Those who do will declare His works and consider what He has done

67:7 – He blesses us that we may fear Him

85:9 – His salvation is near to them

103:11 – His lovingkindness (grace) is as high as the heavens are above the earth to them

103:13 – He has a father's compassion for them

103:17 – His lovingkindness is from everlasting to everlasting to those who do

111:5 – He feeds them and remembers His covenant to them forever

111:10 – It is the beginning of wisdom for them

115:11 – He is their help and their defender

115:13 – He blesses them

119:63 – He makes them companions in fellowship

119:120 – They fear His judgments

145:19 – He fulfills their desires, and hears their cries and saves them

147:11 – He favors them

Endnotes

[i] Connecting, W Publishing Group, ©1997, pg. 90

[ii] Dallas Willard, The Divine Conspiracy, ©1997, Harper Collins, pg. 135